Supermom
HAS LEFT THE BUILDING

Being a Proverbs 31
Woman in a 21st Century World

BY JUDITH EDWARDS

new
hope
PUBLISHERS

Birmingham, Alabama

New Hope® Publishers
P. O. Box 12065
Birmingham, AL 35202-2065
www.newhopepubl.com

Library of Congress Cataloging-in-Publication Data
Edwards, Judith, 1943-
Supermom has left the building : being a Proverbs 31 woman in a 21st century world / by Judith Edwards.
p. cm.
ISBN 1-56309-772-9 (pbk.)
1. Mothers-Religious life. 2. Motherhood-Religious aspects-Christianity. 3. Mothers in the Bible. 4. Bible. O.T. Proverbs XXXI-Criticism, interpretation, etc. I. Title.
BV4529.18.E39 2004
248.8'431—dc22
2003025675

ISBN: 1-56309-772-9

N044102 • 0404 • 7.5M1

DEDICATION

To Rhonda, Perry, and Nita—

Three children who knew I was not Supermom
but pretended they didn't know,

Who forgave me for trying to be Supermom,

And loved me anyway.

TABLE OF CONTENTS

INTRODUCTION

Look! Up in the sky!

    It's a bird!

        It's a plane!

            It's...Supermom!

Faster than a speeding bullet—

Always on time—never late—usually early, in fact.

    Poised, graceful, always looks like a fashion model.

        Proficiently juggles ten life-roles at one time.

More powerful than a locomotive—

Never lets the realities of life get her down.

    Welcomes all problems, faces them head on and
        comes out a winner.

        Confidently knows "who she is" and "where she
            is going."

Able to leap tall buildings in a single bound—

    Never hesitates because the building is too tall.

    Washes the windows on her way up.

        Always lands, feet first, on the other side.

Supermom—

    is a "good" mother (whatever that means),

        is a "perfect" homemaker (she never burns
            the toast),

            invites visitors to peek into her neat, orderly
            closets.

Supermom would never—

run out of peanut butter or yell at her kids,

    have rings around her bathtub or dust on the base
        boards,

        lock her keys in the car. (While it is running?)

Supermom always—

    checks pockets before doing the laundry,

        is understanding, patient, kind,

            says just the right thing at the right time.

Supermom? I'm afraid I'll never qualify. As for speeding bullets...the fastest I ever moved was the time my son put a frog on my shoulder. "Powerful" is more comparable to a ten-speed bike than a locomotive. Leap tall buildings? How about tall stacks of dirty laundry?

Oh, every day we hear all those statements that subtly tell us we should be perfect, tempting us to fall into the supermom trap.

- "Karen's mom *made* her dress for the play."
- "My dear, how *do* you manage to work all day and still keep such a—uh—tidy house?"
- "Mom, fix the zipper in my backpack while I eat a sandwich. What do you mean, no bread?"
- "We just knew you were the perfect one to teach this class. You know what they say—if you want something done, ask a busy person."
- "Now you take Aunt Loly...you could eat off her floor."
- "Marsha's such a *good* mother. She's a Boy Scout Den Mother, you know."
- "Mom will be glad to sponsor the choir trip."
- "So you're taking early retirement to take care of your grandchildren. How noble!"
- "My daughter-in-law and I are best friends. What about you?"

In reality, no mother qualifies for supermom. Oh, we sometimes look at others who claim (or pretend) to be supermoms and convince ourselves that in order to be "good" mothers we need to somehow fit that role. We put pressure on ourselves to achieve this illusory goal, then find it hard to forgive ourselves when we don't measure up to our own expectations, or those that we allow the world to impose on us.

Motherhood has no age or generation limits. A mother is a mother, whether she is a young working mother breastfeeding her infant, a soccer mom driving a mini-van around town, a mother of a teen watching her hair turn gray overnight, a mother at her daughter's wedding, a grandmother at a piano recital—when we become mothers, our lives change forever. Mothers of all ages are potential contestants in the Supermom Pageant.

Just a few days ago I heard a news reporter say that a major cause of depression and frustration for women today is that they are caught in the trap of trying to be supermoms. That afternoon my neighbor told me her daughter and two children were "moving back home." Overwhelmed with her changing roles, she sighed, "They think I'm supermom; I just want to be grandma." Everywhere I look I see women trying to win the title of World's Greatest Supermom, then feeling guilty or like a failure when they don't even qualify as a finalist.

ONE MOM'S STORY

Laurie planned the "perfect" trip for herself and her four sons. She had worked out every detail of the itinerary. She would drive the van over 2,000 miles before the trip ended and include visits with relatives as well as educational and recreational stops. The highlight of the two-week trip was to be a boat ride to an island just off the California coast where they could watch whales. On Monday she bought the tickets, confirmed the 6:45 A.M. departure time, and put four excited boys to bed. Tuesday morning came too soon, so they were running just a little behind Laurie's planned schedule, but they were still in good shape. That is, until she missed her exit off the freeway. In the process of finding another exit and retracing her steps, she made a wrong turn. They arrived at the dock at 7:03 A.M.—just in time to watch the boat leave without them.

The boys adjusted, but Laurie couldn't forgive herself. For several hours she felt physically ill because she had made such a mistake and had, in her thinking, "ruined the trip for everyone." About noon she called her own mother to report, "Mama, I'm just going to have to admit that I'm not a supermom."

Believing that we must be perfect is one of the biggest hindrances to being and becoming what we should be. Why do we think we must be supermoms? Is it what we think we must do in order to please someone else, or perhaps to prove something to ourselves?

Most of us have the opportunity to grow gently into the knowledge that we are not, and do not have to be, supermoms. Lois, a coworker of mine, didn't have that opportunity. She was a career woman with no children until, at the ages of 47 and 48, she and her husband adopted two preschoolers. Talk about a paradigm shift! The children moved into their house on the Saturday before Easter Sunday. One year later she and I were visiting by phone. She asked about things at the office, then asked what else I was doing. I told her about my latest cross-stitch project, then said, "I'm also writing a book—'Supermom Has Left the Building.'"

"The *building*? Supermom has left the *planet*!" she exclaimed.

Webster defines a myth as a "person or thing having only an imaginary or unverifiable existence." I have come to the conclusion through observation and many years of personal experience that supermoms are not real; they are mythological beings. I have also discovered a number of myths about super-mothering that I'd like to explore with you. So throw back your cape, find a comfortable chair, and enjoy the ride!

CHAPTER ONE

Supermoms

HAVE RHYMING SOCKS

How many times, I wonder, have we come upon a truly great event, perhaps a turning point in our lives, and never even known we were there until we were gone—until the moment had passed? Come with me to one such moment in my life.

It was a Monday morning, for these things usually happen on Mondays. Our son was a cooperative child and normally tolerant of his mother, who thought she had to be a supermom, though I am sure I had never said it out loud. I can still see Perry, age seven, standing in the kitchen doorway holding up for my review a blue sock, a green sock, a gray sock, and four white socks with respective stripes of yellow, red, purple, and black.

"Mama," Perry asked patiently as I looked up from the eggs I was scrambling, "do I have *any* socks that rhyme?" Perry left for school wearing two of the white socks, one with a black stripe and one with a brown. I spent the next hour in his bedroom, cleaning out his dresser, searching the bottom of his closet, pulling all kinds of things from beneath his bed, and turning the toy box upside down in search of at least one sock that would rhyme with at least one other sock. I did find the green and blue ones, and also found a tan one with two brown stripes. It didn't rhyme either!

Later that morning, as I sat down with a second cup of coffee, I came to my own profound (at least to me) understanding of the basic philosophy of motherhood. Supermoms have rhyming socks. The distinction between *ordinary* and *super* lies not in whether or not one's beds are made each morning, how well one's children behave, what school functions one attends or sponsors, nor how many nights one makes hot bread in her bread machine. Performing with grace the delicate art of juggling career, home, and family is not the deciding factor. The ultimate test is to be found in the laundry basket. And I had failed miserably. My son's socks didn't rhyme.

By the end of the morning I had filled a bag with socks in which there was no poetry at all. And that was not all I had done. I had learned some important lessons about being a supermom. Or *not* being a supermom, as the case may be.

And it was okay! Perhaps that was the most shocking thought of all! My son had actually walked out the door wearing socks that didn't rhyme, and I had been set free from my self-inflicted delusions that I had to be the "perfect" mother. In fact, I was coming close to discovering that there is no such creature as a supermom.

I soon realized that I was not alone. I seriously doubt that there is any woman who has always had, under every circumstance, socks that rhyme. The unsolved mystery of the disappearing sock haunts every person who has ever done laundry. The eternal question remains: what happens to the missing sock? Does the washing machine eat it? Does a one-legged gremlin steal it? Wherever it goes, that one lone sock is all that stands in the way of any of us reaching total achievement of the elusive goal—to be supermoms.

On that significant Monday morning I made two discoveries and a decision. *Discovery #1*: Supermoms have rhyming socks. My socks didn't rhyme, therefore I was not a supermom. *Discovery #2*: No one else has socks that always rhyme, so supermoms are a myth. *Decision*: I will do and be the best I can, but if I fall short of super perfection, that's okay. I'll survive! (And so will my family.)

THE PROVERBS 31 MOM

Just when I thought I had this all figured out, I was asked to lead a women's retreat. The Scripture I was to use? Proverbs 31. You know—the original supermom chapter. There I was, face to face with a mother who worked, sewed, made decisions, planted a field. She pleased her husband; her children were exemplary; she dressed like a queen. She got up early and worked until late at night. I instinctively disliked and was intimidated by this woman who was creative, organized, efficient, confident, and compassionate.

However, as I continued to read and study, I found myself becoming friends with her. I think perhaps her name was Miriam. I even came to her defense when I heard a preacher make this statement in his Mother's Day sermon: "Of course we realize this woman was a composite of all women. No woman could possibly fill all those roles and do it so well." Here was a lady who had many if not all of the same roles as I did, and she filled them graciously and with charm. This woman and women today have a great deal in common. "No woman could possibly fill all the roles" that most women today are expected, often required, to fill.

The writer of the Book of Proverbs began by saying, "Listen, my son, to your father's instruction and do not forsake your mother's teaching" (Proverbs 1:8). Then the last chapter of the book begins by telling us that the wise words about the chapter 31 woman came to King Lemuel from his mother. Lemuel (meaning devoted to God) was probably another name for Solomon. If that be so, remember that his mother was Bathsheba. She certainly knew the power of a woman to influence and affect a man's life for good or bad! (See 2 Samuel 11.)

Tell me, what advice would you give to your son if you knew that he was going to someday be king? I like to picture the young man, sitting on the floor at his mother's feet, looking into her eyes. Bathsheba warns her son against drinking wine or strong drink, advises him to speak out for the poor and unfortunate, to judge righteously, and to defend the rights of the needy and afflicted (Proverbs 31:1–9). Then she says, "Son, I am going to tell you some things to look for when you choose a wife."

The remainder of the chapter is, in Hebrew, a beautiful acrostic poem describing the virtues of a noble woman. The first verse begins with the first letter of the Hebrew alphabet, followed in turn by the remaining 21 letters. Whether or not these last verses are a part of her words to her son, they are certainly an appropriate ending to such a practical book of wisdom. If you read between the lines, you realize that this special, God-fearing woman was also an unusually wise and gifted teacher.

Almost three thousand years later, we still look to the woman in the poem as a "model" wife and mother. I wonder how many Mother's Day sermons have been preached about her? She was human and surely had her own assortment of faults. Yet outwardly she was kind, gracious, and organized. Inwardly she was godly, loving, and righteous. Truly a woman with these attributes is worthy of praise (Proverbs 31:30).

I began asking myself some questions. What does this lady of Proverbs 31 know that I don't know? What makes her so special? How can I, a 21st century mother, become more fully the woman God created me to be? I discovered that my new friend Miriam had much to teach me about coping in today's hurried, worried, fast-paced world. Was she really a super-mom? Perhaps, but I rather think that she was just an ordinary woman trying to do her best. At any rate, she taught me some invaluable lessons that I have revisited frequently as I have lived out my role as mother.

Many mornings have come and gone since the one when Perry's socks didn't rhyme. Many lost socks, many unmade beds, many loaves of cold, store-bought bread. I now have grandchildren, and I am sure they also sometimes wear socks that don't rhyme. Oh yes, even as mother to adult children, I still find myself trying to be a supermom. I still fall into the trap of thinking I am responsible for everyone else's happiness and comfort. I sometimes think that perhaps the temptation to be "super" is even greater as our children become adults, for we know they can see clearly our mistakes and weaknesses.

I always found and still find that sooner or later, in one way or another, I come up short of the goal. But I really found free-dom when I admitted to myself that I am not required to be a supermom. The requirements for "supermom-ing" were ones I had imposed on myself, or allowed others or the world to impose on me. God doesn't want me to be supermom. God wants me to be the best *me* I can be, with my life centered on Him.

As a reformed supermom, I've learned a lot of lessons! A few things I've learned the easy way; most have come with a price tag. Some lessons grew from an experience with my own mother and my children; some are sprouts that grew from a seed planted by a conversation with a friend. Sometimes I couldn't apply the lessons until later, when I reflected on the experience. And sometimes I just had to hold my head in my hands and admit, "I blew it. I'll try to do better next time."

I invite you to join me as we look at some lessons the Proverbs 31 woman, whom I'll call Miriam, can teach us about mothering. Instead of an in-depth, scholarly study of the 31st chapter of Proverbs, this is rather one mother's look at this proverbial woman through 21st century eyes. We will expose some of those laborious myths that can make really great but terribly average women feel like failures. (Floors so clean you could eat on them? Hel-lo! Who wants to eat spaghetti off someone's floor?) I will share with you some of the very real things I have learned about accepting myself. Some experiences are practical, some comical, some downright hilarious, some sad, some mundane—but all are threads that together weave a rug that pictures the great adventure of mothering.

Throughout the book you will become acquainted with three fantastic kids who have known all their lives that I am far from being a supermom. Oh, they often told me I was the greatest, to make me feel good. They also frequently assumed the responsibility of keeping me humble, reminding me that without a doubt, I was *not* a supermom!

Rhonda, our first-born, somehow survived (as do most first children) in spite of my efforts to be the "perfect" mother, determined to present her to the world as a "perfect" child. Two years later along came Perry, who somehow survived all my attempts to correct the mistakes I had made with Rhonda. By the time Nita completed the trio three years later, I was beginning to suspect that I would never have a perfect child, and I certainly would never be a perfect mother, so I just relaxed and enjoyed her! My three children are adults now, and I've had the delight of watching Rhonda, my child, hold my first grandchild.

You will also meet Dalton, the patient man who has stood beside me all these years, encouraging me to keep trying to leap over those tall stacks of laundry! He knows I'm not supermom, but he pretends he doesn't know. He has truly been the "wind beneath my wings."

Through it all, we've had a great time. We've laughed a lot; we've cried quite a bit, too. We've disagreed and worried and argued and forgiven. We've said "I love you" and "I'm sorry" and "Thank you" more times than could be counted. Then we laughed some more. I may not have been a supermom, but I sure had a lot of fun just being an ordinary mother.

I invite you to go on a supermom myth hunt with me. If, as you read, you find one word, one phrase, one thought that causes you to smile, to wipe a tear, to remember, to glimpse a new color in life's prism, to reflect on your own journey, to forgive yourself, to laugh out loud—then I have written and you have read for that reason. Perhaps you will find freedom to become more of what God intended you to be, and less of the supermom others think you should be. Perhaps you will see a new portrait of yourself, or of others, that helps you decide which road to take, which flower to pick, which fragrance to savor, which moment to cherish.

CHAPTER TWO

Supermoms

COOK BREAKFAST

You don't believe me? It says so in Proverbs 31:15! "She gets up before daylight to prepare food for her family and for her servants" (CEV). Still not convinced? Let's try other versions—Eugene Peterson says, "She's up before dawn, preparing breakfast for her family" (*The Message*), and even the King James Version says, "She riseth also while it is yet night, and giveth meat to her household."

Does this mean that mothers who don't fix biscuits, gravy, and hash browns every morning are breaking the eleventh commandment? I don't think so! At least, I don't think so *now*. Stay with me while I explain what I mean.

Sociologists have given my generation a lot of titles, but I have added one to the list—the Supermom Generation. When I was in school the home economics textbooks told us all the things a "good" wife should do. And of course, being the first family member out of bed in the mornings was a given. Every member of the family should be sent out into the cold, cruel world with a warm breakfast in their tummies! There were all kinds of things a mother could do to make her home a castle where her husband, "the king," could come for refuge after a hard day at the office. Most of those *great* (really?) words of advice I've long since forgotten, but I do recall a few bits of that well-intentioned—although antiquated!—wisdom.

Just before it is time for father, wearing his suit and tie and carrying a black leather briefcase, to walk through the front door in the evening, mother should wash the faces of her little darlings, dress them in clean clothes, and put bows in the princesses' hair. Then she should comb her own hair, freshen her makeup, and don a nicely ironed housedress. She should greet him at the door with a pleasant smile and *never* complain about the tedious day she had spent completing her domestic duties! I distinctly remember reading in some book or article that sautéing some onions just before hubby came home would give the pleasant aroma of cooking food, creating an atmosphere of anticipation for the meal (gourmet, of course) that was in store.

I'm sure you've already picked up on my sarcasm as well as several pre-21st century ideas. In the first place, today's daddy is probably wearing a polo shirt or an open-necked shirt beneath his pullover sweater. Instead of a briefcase, he is carrying a small binder that holds his PDA and cell phone. The children are probably at day care or soccer practice, because mom herself has either been at work all day or isn't home yet, still shuttling those soccer players from one field to another. Does any woman even own a "housedress" any more? If I've worn a dress to work (notice I said *if*), the first thing I do when I get home is put on my jeans. And about those sautéed onions— now where did I put that frying pan? I can hardly find it!

The TV family of a generation ago—families like the Cleavers of *Leave It To Beaver*—are so unbelievable today that we laugh at the images. The stereotypical family was a mother, father, and 2.7 children. (Did you ever wonder about that .7 child?) They lived in a white house in the suburbs, drove a station wagon, and all ate dinner together at 6:00 P.M. every evening. Roles were defined: Daddy was the wage earner, mother the homemaker, and the children's lives centered around the family. Even comedies like "Happy Days" and "I Love Lucy" portrayed this same family structure.

What happened? Times changed! When our son Perry married Kelley, they were both still in college. Kelley told me one day that they didn't have any pink or blue jobs at their house. I liked that idea! And I realized that "pink and blue" defined my generation very well.

We were the generation of stay-at-home moms, not so much because it was a lifestyle choice but because we were told that's what a "good" mother did. Mothers worked outside their homes because of necessity, not choice. They often felt they had to explain or justify their decision to enter the working world. Then, as so often happens, the pendulum swung in the other direction. Today the mother who chooses to be a "stay-at-home mom" feels she must defend her decision, or at least give the reasons she made this choice. The question a generation ago was, "Why does she work outside her home?" Today the question is, "Why *doesn't* she work outside her home?"

Did you ever buy a sweatshirt with the label "one size fits all"? Ha! One size may fit *some*, or might even occasionally fit *most*—but never *all*! What is right for one woman, one family, cannot become the formula for all others. I want to believe that our 21st century society has moved, or at least is moving, in the right direction away from labeling mothers as either "working" or "stay-at-home." You may have seen the minivan advertisement with a caption that reads something like: "Who in the world came up with the term 'stay-at-home mom'?"

I wish for every mother that she could find and fill the role that fits her best. Marta is one of those "stay-at-home" moms who homeschools her five children. Becky travels a lot in her job; her husband is happy to be Mr. Mom. Debra gives piano lessons from her home, and Cathy sells cosmetics. Beth is a single mom who works because she has to; Kara is a physician, fulfilling her childhood dream. No matter what her choice, all mothers can follow the scriptural admonition that whatever our hands find to do, we are to do it with all our might (Ecclesiastes 9:10), or as Peterson says in *The Message*, "Each day is God's gift. It's all you get in exchange for the hard work of staying alive. Make the most of each one! Whatever turns up, grab it and do it. And heartily!" (Ecclesiastes 9:9–10).

I was very young when I got my first MAMA degree. (I realize *now* how young I was—at the time I thought I was quite mature, thank you!) I fell headlong into that supermom trap, and believe me, the trap can close tightly around the wants-to-do-it-right mother! It's hard to break away. And after all, in my defense, most of the models I saw were wanna-be super-moms, and the advice I received went right along with that illusion. I sincerely thought I had to be the kind of wife and mother that my high school home economics book and Mrs. Murphy (my home economics teacher) described. I tried! Honest, I did! And when I didn't quite succeed, I felt I should just try harder.

Of course, in retrospect, I think I always wanted to try a different road. I'll never forget the day our home ec class cooked breakfast. The class was divided into "kitchen groups," and each group was to make the same thing. I don't recall anything else on the menu, but I know I was in charge of making hot cocoa. Mrs. Murphy explained at great length that before making cocoa, we should mix the powdered cocoa and sugar with just a bit of water, then add it to the milk. Otherwise, the dry ingredients would lump.

You've already guessed the next part of the story, I'm sure. I poured the cold milk into the pan then scooped in the cocoa and sugar. In horror I looked at the brown clumps floating in the pan. What to do? Giggling as only teenage girls can do, we grabbed an eggbeater and quickly took care of those lumps, leaving beautiful, creamy chocolate milk in the pan.

When Mrs. Murphy came to inspect our work, she called everyone over to our kitchen. I can still hear her words: "Now class, I want you to come over here and look at Judith's cocoa. She made it just like I said. See how creamy and smooth it is?" The girls in my kitchen nearly passed out from suppressed laughter!

I learned some lessons for living that day that were more important than how to make cocoa. They apply to mothering as well as cooking. Sometimes we just don't quite make the grade. Sometimes we forget, or get in a hurry, or just don't take the time to do what we know we should do. Thank heavens for eggbeaters! There's usually a solution. And there's usually a way to fix most problems. Even when there are lumps in life, it's not the end of the world. Someone else has said that when life gives you a lemon, you should make lemonade. I'd say when your cocoa lumps, it's time to grab an eggbeater!

SUPERMOM MYTHS

Does the supermom really fix breakfast every morning? My mother did, and I thought I had to be up and at least available to take orders, even if I hadn't prepared a meal. Wasn't that one of those "pink" jobs that I was "supposed" to do? So I made it to the kitchen most every morning while our children were still at home, sometimes the in-control chef, sometimes a short order cook, sometimes setting the cold cereal on the table. Three cheers (and two cups of coffee) for supermom!

Then my breakfast-eaters grew up and had homes of their own. I shall never forget the night I spent at Rhonda's home when her first two children were in daycare. I had never been there before on a weekday morning. While Rhonda was in her bedroom getting ready for work, Jeremy and Jenna, ages three and five, dressed themselves and then came into the kitchen where I was drinking coffee. Without comment, they took their cereal from the cabinet, got their own bowls and spoons, and sat down beside me to eat. I was amazed! They did it all by themselves! And quite capably and matter-of-factly at that!

Reality check—what is breakfast? Isn't it the meal that gets us ready for the day ahead? Could it be that by teaching her children to do things for themselves, to be independent, Rhonda was preparing them for the *days* ahead in a better way than I had done by doing all the work for my children?

SPIRITUAL FOOD

The Amplified Bible adds an important word to this 15th verse of Proverbs 31: "She rises while it is yet night and gets [*spiritual*] food for her household." Here's a new thought—perhaps the "breakfast" our families really need is spiritual nourishment. Perhaps, instead of lumpy oatmeal, they need to be equipped for the unknown lumps in the road ahead. Perhaps, in addition to bacon and eggs, it is self-confidence they need. Perhaps, after coming through a dark night, they need to know that the Bread of Life is available, that the Light of the World will be waiting at the end of the day.

Okay, so much for breakfast. There are other meals in the day, too! Does a supermom cook these meals as well? I did enjoy cooking when my children were at home—especially during their teenage years when the kids ate anything and everything. Cooking in an empty nest, however, takes on new dimensions.

Recently, at Christmastime while we were in the process of remodeling our kitchen, Dalton bought me a new stove. My friend Susan asked, "But why would he get you something you'll never use?"

Dalton says that when he wants to hide a gift for me, he puts it in the oven. He knows I'll never look there! But I do cook—honestly. Frozen entrees, salads already cut and mixed, Hamburger Helper, all kinds and varieties of pastries and breads, dozens of salad dressings and prepared sauces—with all these options, even women like me can find something to cook. What fun it has been to watch additions to the grocery store shelves during my mothering years.

Another verse in Proverbs 31 also refers to food. "She buys imported foods, brought by ship from distant ports" (Proverbs 31:14 TLB). Miriam could have run down to a market booth and purchased a couple of cold dead fish for supper. Instead she met the ships as they came in from far-off places and purchased from them foods that would bring delight to her family.

Mealtime can be an important time for a family. Though I was an only child, I have great growing-up memories of my parents and me as we sat at our gray chrome dining table eating the meat and produce from our farm. Mealtime conversations ranged from stories of their childhoods to discussions of current affairs to religious topics. I wonder how much of my childhood understanding of theology was formed over fried chicken and gravy.

For almost 35 years our family has enjoyed meals around a large round oak table that had been in Dalton's family from the time he was seven. I remember many Thanksgivings, Christmases, and other family gatherings at Hammah's (Dalton's mother) when the table was covered with all kinds of goodies. When Hammah died, all of her eight children wanted that one piece of furniture, so they drew straws.

Dalton, the baby (excuse me, youngest) of the children, won! Ever since, that table has been the special meeting place for our family. When we have made moves, we always had to find a house with a dining area that would accommodate the table.

I served many unusual meals on that table while we lived on the Navajo reservation in northern New Mexico, where we were missionaries. In addition to the many Navajo friends who ate there, we had a steady flow of other guests. Once, while visiting us, my mother said, "You don't have to go anywhere. The whole world comes to your door!" State and national denominational workers, tourists visiting that beautiful part of the world, friends from years before who took this opportunity to tour Navajoland—she was right! The whole world came to my door—and sat at our table!

JESUS AT MEALTIME

We have a great example when we think about eating together: mealtime was important to Jesus. The Bible records several meals Jesus ate, many of them with companions whose names would not have been found on the society pages of the *Jerusalem Journal*. For example: After Matthew the tax collector became a follower of Jesus, he invited Jesus and His disciples to a meal in his home. The religious leaders, who were surely the keepers of the social register, asked the disciples, "Why does He eat and drink with tax collectors and [notorious] sinners?" (Mark 2:16 AMP).

One evening, while surrounded by a "crowd" of people, Jesus' disciples came to Him and said something like, "We're a long way from the closest cafeteria and it's getting late—even McDonald's will soon be closed. You'd better send these people back into town so they can eat." And what did Jesus do? He took five loaves and two fish and fed all the people, with some leftovers for lunch the next day! (See Matthew 14:15–21.)

Jesus even included mealtime when He told a story. When Andy, the prodigal son returned home, the father didn't just offer him a sandwich and cup of coffee. He killed a calf, barbequed it, and invited the whole village to the celebration (Luke 15:11–32). (Did you not know the son's name was Andy? It's right there in verse 20 in the King James Version— "Andy arose, and came to his father.")

I would like to have been there when Jesus had breakfast with Peter (John 21:9–14) beside the Sea of Tiberias. Peter was feeling pretty low about this time—Jesus, his teacher and friend, had been crucified. On top of that, Peter had done a terrible thing—he had denied even knowing this wonderful man. He cut off the ear of the high priest's servant when the mob came to take Jesus, but when the going got tough he didn't even stand up for Jesus. Then along came Jesus—the risen Lord—and cooked some fish for Peter. How delicious that fish must have tasted to the forgiven man.

There is yet another time the resurrected Jesus revealed Himself to His companions at a meal. He walked along the road with a couple from Emmaus, discussing the events of the day. I think this was a husband and wife team, on their way back to their home after witnessing things they could not even comprehend. It wasn't until they "broke bread together" that they recognized their magnificent guest (Luke 24:13–35).

Jesus used mealtimes as teachable moments—teaching about humility (Luke 14:10–11), about mercy (Luke 14:12–14), about priorities (Luke 10:38–42), about serving others (John 13:4–10). And of course we still celebrate today the last meal He had with His disciples, a time for remembering His great, incomprehensible, sacrificial love for us (Luke 22:14–20).

Even after Jesus passed the work on to those who followed Him, mealtime was important. The new church members ate together, rejoicing in their new faith (Acts 2:46–47). After Saul was blinded by the light on the road to Damascus, Ananias spoke to him and, "Something like fish scales fell from Saul's eyes, and he could see. He got up and was baptized. Then he ate and felt much better" (Acts 9:18–19 CEV).

And guess what? If we are His followers, we're going to join Him at the best meal yet! "Look at me. I stand at the door. I knock. If you hear me call and open the door, I'll come right in and *sit down to supper with you.* Conquerors will sit alongside me at the head table, just as I, having conquered, took the place of honor at the side of my Father. That's my gift to the conquerors!" (Revelation 3:20–21 *The Message*).

You know, I'm glad that this Proverbs 31 mother, giving her son advice on what virtues to look for in a wife, mentioned food. Meal planning, preparation, and consumption are basic parts of our everyday lives. Three meals a day, 365 days a year—let's see, that makes 1,095 meals a year, not counting snacks. Perhaps this verse should remind us to be thankful for the food we have to eat, and for the hungry mouths we have to feed. We should remember that even simple, daily, sometimes monotonous tasks can be a way of saying to our families, "I love you."

CHAPTER THREE

Supermoms

HAVE MAIDS

As soon as the breakfast dishes were stored in the dishwasher and the milk put back in the refrigerator, the Proverbs 31 woman, whom we call Miriam, turns her attention to another matter—assigning "her maids their tasks" (verse 15 AMP). Or as Ken Taylor says, planning "the day's work for her servant girls" (TLB).

The first time I read this I thought, *Yeah, sure! Now I understand. Easy for her to do all these things—easy to be a supermom—she had servant girls to help her.* Then I realized—so do I! I have a whole house full of them, don't you? As I introduce you to some of mine, you must understand that I name everything—well, almost everything. So of course, most of my servant girls have names. And Rachel, one of my servant girls, is helping me write this book.

When I bought my first computer I knew she needed a name because we would be spending a lot of time together. My pastor had named his computer Baruch, the name of Jeremiah's scribe (see Jeremiah 36). That was clever, but it just didn't fit my situation. Somehow I couldn't see myself saying, "I spent the day with Baruch." So I called in my advisors. Perry said, "Well, let's see—how long have you been writing?"

I counted back to the first article I had published. "Fourteen years."

"That's easy then. Name her Rachel." And Rachel she became. (You do remember the story from Genesis 29, don't you? How long did Jacob work for Laban so he could have Rachel as his wife? If you said 14 years, you were right.)

Even though Rachel has been reincarnated several times, her name has never changed. Of course, I had to have another name for my laptops—they have all been Ruth, living up to her promise that "whither thou goest, I will go" (Ruth 1:16). Now I have the cutest, tiniest laptop you've ever seen. At Rhonda's suggestion, she is Baby Ruth.

When Perry and Kelley were beginning their seminary education, I knew the best servant girl I could give them was a computer. After finding the right one, I packaged it carefully and mailed it with this note inside: "Hello! I am Isaiah. Your mother said, 'I need someone to go help my kids while they are in school.' And I replied, 'Here am I. Send me.'"

I have many other servants, of course. Lucille is my clothes dryer. She always decides to quit when I have sheets to dry because company is coming in a couple of hours. On more than one occasion some child had to wear damp socks to school because they didn't quite get dry. (No, they probably didn't rhyme, either.) Lucille never leaves at a convenient time, living up to her reputation in the Kenny Rogers song where she got her name: "You picked a fine time to leave me, Lucille."

But in spite of the fact that she sometimes has an attitude, Lucille is still a valued part of our family. In less than an hour a load of laundry is dry and most of the contents are ironed. When I get impatient, I remember that doing the laundry was an all-day affair for my mother. The washing was done in a wringer washing machine, and then she hung the clothes on the line to dry. When at the end of the day they were dry (assuming there was neither sandstorm nor rain that day) she brought them in, sprinkled many of them, and put them in a plastic bag to be ironed the next day. It was hard, time-consuming work. Yes, Lucille is a servant girl whom I appreciate.

Then there's Lucy, my dishwasher. I do love Lucy! When Lucy the First came to live with us, I had a very small kitchen, so Lucy had to be portable. There was no place for Lucy to live except right in the middle of the kitchen. She was always in the way and had to be rolled from place to place so I could get to the sink, back to the stove, then to the refrigerator. Did I complain? No way. As I walked by I would pat her lid and say, "Don't worry. That's just fine. I still appreciate you."

I think you get the idea—I have maids. If you want an exercise in thankfulness, take a minute to look around your house. How many servant girls live in your house? Consider all those electric appliances we use every day—coffee pots, toasters, curling irons, vacuum cleaners, and microwave ovens, to name just a few. Even the electricity that powers them is a blessing we take for granted until we are without it.

Norma, one of my Navajo friends who lived on the reservation, lived in a hogan with her four children. She not only had no electricity in her home, she didn't even have running water. Her husband hauled water to their home in barrels in the back of their pickup. I shall never forget one of the days she was visiting in my home. She watched as I started a load of washing, then said, "It must be so nice to have a washing machine in your house."

Our houses are full of non-electric maids, too. I have a picture in our family album of my grandmother sitting outside her house in front of a black kettle over an open fire; she was making soap. A quick review of even the contents in our kitchen cabinets will remind us of many food conveniences we often take for granted. And we must not forget those servant girls who help us so much with communication—I believe their names are Page R., Ann Swering-Machine, E. Mail, and of course those two Phone girls, Cell and Cordless. Yes, we have servant girls in abundance—servant girls our friend Miriam never knew existed.

CHILDREN AND CHORES

Our children are pretty good "servant girls," too. Wait a minute—that sounded terrible, didn't it? We don't think of them as servants or maids, but children can and should help at home. Now getting them to *do* that is another story. But the idea is great!

Like most other mothers, I tried all kinds of gimmicks and strategies to motivate, entice, and encourage my children to help. I began when they were small, asking them to help by picking up their toys and clothes. One day, when Rhonda and Perry were four and two, I wanted them to clean their room. Deciding to use the positive, pleasant, diplomatic approach, I said cheerfully, "I'd like you guys to clean your room if you don't mind." (I was still in my supermom mode, in case you hadn't noticed.)

"We mind, Mama." They were just as pleasant as I had been. Okay, so I tried a more direct approach next time.

When Shirley and Don arrived at their daughter's home, granddaughter Chelsea was playing in the middle of the living room floor. Mother had been trying to get her to pick up the toys for several minutes, knowing company was coming.

"Papa Don, come play with me," Chelsea sweetly requested as soon as they walked through the door. Of course Papa Don sat beside her on the floor and followed her instructions of "Put this here. Put that over there." In just a couple of minutes Chelsea was gone.

"Chelsea, pick up your toys!" Mother demanded.

"Papa Don has to help me."

"Why?" Mother asked.

"Because he played with them, too."

Children sometimes let us in on a secret—they are just as smart as, or maybe smarter than, we are.

As they grow older, so does the challenge of getting them to help. I thought perhaps creativity would help. I made charts on which they could put smiling face stickers when they did their chores. I seem to recall that we bought only one package of stickers, and they lasted a long time. We tried the point system—one point if you do your chores, two if you do something you weren't asked to do, and negative points if you didn't do what you were supposed to do. That one didn't last long, either. Our math formulas never seemed to correspond.

Then one day Patti and I came up with the bright idea of a "sorry-about-that box" for our children. When personal items—shoes, toys, books, whatever—were not put up and I found them, they ended up in the sorry-about-that box. The owner had to pay a nickel to redeem them. That worked well for Rhonda and Perry, both of whom were learning the value of money. Nita, however, was preparing for a life of luxury. More than once I said, "Nita, if you don't pick up your shoes I'm going to put them in the sorry-about-that box."

"Okay, I'll go get my nickel," was her usual reply. So much for the sorry-about-that box.

When they were teenagers, quite by accident I discovered a way to get them to clean their rooms. It all began one Saturday morning when I threatened, "Clean your room today, or I'm going to clean it on Monday." They didn't, and I did!

I found things I wasn't supposed to, threw away things they wanted to keep, and created all kinds of disturbance in their private domains. From then on, all I had to do was promise that if they didn't clean, I would.

Sometimes we wonder if the battle to get children of any age to help with household chores is worth the effort, but there is another, and possibly more important, reason for requiring their assistance. They are learning a lot of things while they are sharing the work responsibilities—things like how to clean and organize. They are learning self-control and that they should take responsibility for themselves. I've never owned but have seen plaques in homes that read something similar to this: "You drop it, you pick it up. You eat off it, you wash it. You sleep in it, you make it in the morning." Something as simple as putting their own dirty dishes in the dishwasher not only helps with clean-up; it teaches that everyone has a part in helping.

PERFECTIONIST MAMA

I've found not only for me, but for many other mothers as well, one of the primary reasons we don't insist that our children help more is that we are perfectionists. It is usually easier, faster, and better to do the jobs ourselves. So what if every corner of the comforter on the bed isn't exactly straight? So what if there's still a little dust on one end of the coffee table—it will soon be joined by more dust. So what if the towels aren't folded exactly as you would fold them?

My daughter Rhonda taught me one of those painful lessons that I mentioned earlier. She wanted to help me prepare a meal for company, and was stirring something that was cooking on the stove. The pan was full, and she splashed just a little over the edge of the pan. I took the spoon from her and said, "If you can't do it right, just don't do it." I reached for the handle of the pan and—you guessed it—tipped the pan and spilled most of the contents. Quietly, almost under her breath, Rhonda said, "I'm glad you did that." It was one of those moments when you wish you could hit the delete button and take back those unthinking words, but they had been spoken. And she had taught me so many good lessons. I hugged her, apologized, and gave her back the spoon.

Rhonda now manages an office and has several people who work with her. Recently one evening as we talked on the phone, she told me how frustrated she was with an inefficient, imperfect co-worker. I listened awhile then said, "In other words, if you can't do it right, just don't do it." We both had a good laugh, and she said, "That's right!" I think she was a bit more tolerant when she went to work the next day.

Andrea was telling me about her struggles with her daughter, who has a learning disability. She wanted Carla to learn how to work, but it was an uphill, daily battle. Carla's room was always a disaster area, and when she was told to clean it, she had no idea how to go about the task. She would stay in her room several minutes looking at the mountains of "stuff," then burst into frustrated tears.

Andrea learned how to help Carla, and the same approach has helped and still helps me when I have any monumental task to accomplish. She calmly went into the room with Carla and instructed her to pick up one item. Just one. "Now, what do you want to do with that book?" Carla put it on her bookshelf. Next item—a candy wrapper. "And where does that go?" Into the trash, of course. And so it went for about 30 minutes. Carla could see bite-size pieces instead of the monstrous mountain she was trying to climb. I thought of the question, "How do you eat an elephant?" The answer, of course, is one bite at a time.

As they help with work at home, kids can be proud of their accomplishments. During their summer break recently,

Rhonda's two daughters asked if they could paint their rooms. I don't know that I would have been brave enough to turn them loose with paint and brushes, but Rhonda gave them instructions, helped them buy the paint, then turned it over to them. They not only painted their rooms, they painted the whole house. They are so proud of the results. And of course, *they* are the ones who insist and help to see that the freshly-painted rooms stay clean.

PLANNING YOUR WORK

Verse 15 of Proverbs 31 reminds us—more important than *having* maids was organizing or planning their work. I've discovered that the emphasis should be on *planning the day's work* for all those servant girls I have. When I am organized, I don't have to try frantically to be supermom; I can relax and enjoy life a bit more when I practice some simple organizational methods.

Our maids are not limited to items we put in cabinets or plug into the wall. What about our financial resources? What about the skills and abilities we have been given that enable us to have these resources? I read somewhere that only five percent of the world's population have more than two pair of shoes in their closet, drive a car, eat three meals a day, and have access to medical help when it is needed. I heard a conference leader say that his mother lived through the depression and he was still suffering from it! Even Americans who don't have much are affluent in comparison to most people. Your garbage disposal eats better than much of the world.

Our friend Miriam, we are told in Proverbs 31:18a, was a businesswoman, or at least she approached her daily tasks with a business mindset. As I read this verse I am interested in the difference in translations and interpretations.

- "She perceiveth that her merchandise is good" (KJV).
- "She tastes and sees that her gain from work [with and for God] is good" (AMP).
- "She knows when to buy or sell" (CEV).
- "She senses the worth of her work" (*The Message*).
- But imagine my delight when I read that "she watches for bargains" in *The Living Bible*! Suddenly I could justify my attraction to garage sales, flea markets, and day-after-Christmas sales. Does "planning the work of our maids" really extend to our finances? I think so.

As soon as we began giving our children an allowance, we taught them that a tithe, or 10 percent, belonged to God. Each week they proudly put their small amount of change into an envelope and placed it in the offering plate during the Sunday morning worship service. We thought they understood the concept of "giving our money to God," but we forgot what literal thinkers children are.

Perry was five when my husband Dalton became pastor of First Baptist Church, Shiprock, New Mexico. Every Monday morning our treasurer, Mr. Bingham, would come to the church, pick up and count the offerings from the day before, then take the money to the bank. Perry watched this process for several months, then one day curiosity got the best of him.

"Mama, I know how we take our money to the church to give it to God, and how Mr. Bingham comes to get it on Monday. But how does Mr. Bingham get the money to God?" Back to the drawing board.

Though I like bargains, I have never liked coupons. I buy a can of coffee with a "redeem immediately" coupon attached to the lid. When I get home I find the coupon, still clinging tenaciously to the lid. I used to keep an envelope filled with coupons in my purse. Every three or four months I would pull them out, throw away the expired ones, and promise myself I would use the others. Then three or four months later, I would throw away another expired group. And when on rare occasions I did remember to use a coupon, I found that the brand I really preferred was already 50 cents cheaper than the brand for which I had a 25-cent coupon.

I didn't realize, however, how vocal I had been about my dislike for coupons until Perry brought home this poem he had written as a school assignment:

> *"My mother sure hates coupons;*
>   *she says they're quite a mess.*
> *Why keep a piece of paper to buy something for less?*
> *Each time she needs to use one*
>   *she searches through her purse*
> *But doesn't find it till she's home, and to make it even worse*
> *She puts one on the counter that's already past the date.*
> *The checker says, 'I'm sorry. It seems that you're too late.'*
> *So if you see my mama with a coupon in her hand*
> *And she looks like she could scream or cry,*
>   *I hope you'll understand."*

Appliances, convenience foods, enough money to buy the things I need, cell phones and email, a minivan to drive to work, and a warm home when I return—how amazingly blessed I am. I have two wishes. First, I hope to be a good steward of these "maids" that are a part of my life. I hope that I will control them, and not allow them to control me. I want to be a good steward of my blessings, using them in a way that would honor my Father, "from whom all blessings flow." Jesus said, "Great gifts mean great responsibilities; greater gifts, greater responsibilities!" (Luke 12:48 *The Message*). If these "things" that fill our lives are gifts, then with them goes the responsibility to use them wisely.

AN ATTITUDE OF GRATITUDE

My second wish is that my life would demonstrate an attitude of gratitude. I pray that I'll never become so accustomed to even the simplest blessings of my life that I fail to be grateful. I shall never forget one cold night when I was awakened by that last glass of iced tea I had during supper. As I crawled out of my warm bed and stumbled toward the bathroom I thought of my friend Karen. That week, after fighting a long battle with ovarian cancer, her kidneys had stopped functioning. With tears in my sleepy eyes I prayed for Karen, then I thanked God that I could get out of my bed and go to the bathroom—thanked Him for my healthy kidneys.

We must keep in perspective the things we own. "Don't love the world's ways. Don't love the world's goods. Love of the world squeezes out love for the Father. Practically everything that goes on in the world—wanting your own way, wanting everything for yourself, wanting to appear important—has nothing to do with the Father. It just isolates you from Him. The world and all its wanting, wanting, wanting is on the way out—but whoever does what God wants is set for eternity" (1 John 2:15-17 *The Message*).

Many of the "servant girls" we enjoy are not absolutely necessary, and they are unavailable for so many mothers around the world. I have been in many one-room Navajo hogans where the only furniture was a stove in the center of the room, an old sofa along one wall, perhaps a chair or two, a small table, and either a bed or stack of blankets that would be spread over the dirt floor at night for sleeping.

I have been in the 10' x 10' home of a mother living in the northern hills of Thailand. The only items in that shelter were the three pots she used to prepare the day's rice, and a few rags she and her three children used as blankets for the night.

I watched children arriving for their school day in

Zimbabwe. Most of them had walked several miles; their only shoes were the heavy calluses that covered the bottoms of their feet. My team left the school to have our lunch in a comfortable house; the children had nothing to eat until they went home at the end of the day. Before they left that evening they came to us to return the pencils we gave them at the start of the day. "Oh, you can keep them," we said casually. The wonder in their eyes at such a gift made me keenly aware of my wasteful habits and the dozens of pencils lying around my house.

What does this have to do with mothering? American mothers in the 21st century have so many things for which we should be thankful. Even in these days when we are so aware of the problems and crises in the world, no mothers before us and few around us have so many conveniences and opportunities. Mothers have the responsibility of teaching children to conserve resources, to be good stewards of their possessions, to use self-control, and to be thankful for what they have.

We should be an example as we express our gratitude instead of complaining. "Be thankful" is a command, not just good advice. We should look for the good in situations instead of the bad, and help our children to do the same. Most parents want their children to have things they could not have when they were children. And most children are quite agreeable with this arrangement. We need to find a balance between giving things to our children and allowing them the joy of discovery for themselves.

Perhaps only a mythical supermom would use her Crock-Pot every day, vacuum three times a week, and simultaneously talk on the phone and curl her hair while her Lucy is washing dishes, a load of clothes is in the washing machine, and her Lucille is drying another load. But every mom can stop and remind herself, "Yes, Norma, it *is* nice to have a washing machine in my home."

CHAPTER FOUR

Supermoms
PLANT GARDENS

Here we go again! The Proverbs 31 woman "looks over a field and buys it, then, with money she's put aside, *plants a garden*" (*The Message*), or as the Amplified Bible says, "she considers a [new] field before she buys or accepts it...with her savings [of time and strength] she *plants fruitful vines* in her vineyard."

I grew up on a farm in eastern New Mexico. Now when I tell you that, you're probably thinking, *Sure, easy for **her** to say that supermoms plant gardens. No doubt not only her thumb but also her pointer finger and pinky are green.* Wrong! While I'm thankful for the lessons I learned there, I'm also thankful that I was the child, and my parents were the adults. I chopped cotton, shocked peanuts, rode the potato setter, pulled broomcorn...and if you understand the language I'm using now, you've had experiences on a farm, too! I milked cows by hand before we had the luxury of electric milking machines, gathered enough eggs to make one awesome omelet, and could even back the hay trailer into the barn just like a truck driver.

I once heard the late evangelist Carlos McCloud, who also grew up on a farm, tell about his call to the ministry. He said that after chopping weeds from each row of cotton he would fall on his knees and plead, "Please, Lord, call me to preach!" I understood what he was saying! When as a high school student I knew God's plan for my life was for me to be a missionary, I certainly didn't say, "But Lord, I wanted to marry a farmer!" You've heard the term "*surrender* to the ministry"? How about *volunteer*? I didn't know where He would send me, but I was sure it would be in a city somewhere. Surely, when He drew my original blueprints, God intended me to be a city girl.

When I married a college student who planned to become a pastor, I moved from the farm to an apartment in our college town. Next, we lived in a big, wonderful city while we attended seminary. We lived in several cities while he served as an Army chaplain. Then God, who is all-wise and all-knowing, and who I suspect has a terrific sense of humor, had another assignment for us. He could have placed us in a city; I would have been content with even a small town. You know, the kind that has grocery stores, and schools, and parks, and traffic lights.

What did He do? He sent us as missionaries to a Navajo reservation right back in our own home state! Our closest neighbors were a Navajo family living in a hogan (the traditional Navajo home) one mile away. Our own house and the church right beside us sat on top of a sandy hill, another mile from the closest paved street. The one tree on top of the hill was in our yard. We were 40 miles from the nearest grocery store, doctor, beauty shop, and shopping mall. Our children were usually the only non-Indians in their classes at school.

And I soon realized that this was not just a rest stop in our journey through life; it became our home for the next seven years! Then for another 16 years we lived in the same general area. I'm so thankful God doesn't tell us the route we will be traveling—we might decide we want a refund on our ticket. After many years of slipping, sliding, and getting stuck on muddy or snow-packed roads, I had a really profound theological insight. The Bible tells us that the streets of heaven are paved with gold; trust me, if they are just *paved*, I'll be happy.

It didn't take me long after our move to the reservation, however, to become captivated by the unique charm and beauty of the area. Shiprock, New Mexico, is a small reservation town in the far northwest corner of the state. Standing in my front door I could look west just a few miles at the Lukachukai (*Beautiful*) mountains in Arizona, north to the Sleeping Ute mountain in Colorado, and between them at the mountain range near Monticello, Utah. Turning just a few degrees to the south I could see the majestic Shiprock itself, a volcanic plug rising 1600 feet above the desert floor.

FARM LIVING

Always a believer that we are supposed to "bloom where we are planted," I set out to make the most of my surroundings. If God wanted me to live in the country, the least I could do was allow my children to experience a taste of farm life. Enter my first solo experiences at gardening. Even though I had grown up knowing the difference between weeds and veggies, it was always my parents who did the actual planning.

So together we planted a garden. Not big by any standards, but considering the sandy New Mexico soil and the necessity of daily watering, it was really a very nice garden. We had—in rows moving from south to north—corn, green beans, tomatoes, watermelon, radishes, onions, cucumbers, and cantaloupe.

Now comes a test for your garden knowledge. If you are a true gardener, your thought was, "You *never* plant cucumbers next to cantaloupe." You're right! But that was something my mother forgot to tell me. As my vines began to bear they presented us with the most unusual vegetable you can imagine— neither cucumber nor cantaloupe. The taste was terrible! But my family, trying to be supportive of their mother and proud of the fruits (or veggies, in this case) of their labors, dutifully took little bites. After washing hers down with a big drink of milk, Nita confessed, "I don't think I like cuke-alopes." No one else did either!

Animals are a part of farm living, and we certainly wanted our children to have that experience. Preschooler Nita watched as our cat Cockle Burr gave birth to five kittens. After each birth Nita would run into the kitchen to tell me, "She made another one!"

Our children had horses, too. Nita's horse was Sugar Babe, a tiny Shetland not much larger than a big dog. Perry's Shetland was gray, and never ran faster than a gentle trot. Combined, these characteristics earned him the name of Granddad. Rhonda rode Red, and Dalton's horse was Apache, a beautiful paint. They all four spent many summer days riding their horses across the prairie behind our house. I remember a Saturday that I stood looking out my kitchen window, watching them come home following an afternoon ride. First was Rhonda on Red, the feisty horse. Then came Dalton and Apache, followed by Nita and Sugar Babe. Far back in the distance came Perry and Granddad. As I watched them I was reminded that the simple pleasures of childhood are such an important part of growing up, and I was glad I could live in a place where my children could have those experiences. (You have taken note, haven't you, that I did not have a horse? That's okay; I didn't feel left out!)

We also had dogs. And dogs. And dogs. Nita and Perry were our animal lovers. Perry adopted Spotty, a black and white "Heinz 57" who stopped by for a visit soon after we arrived in Shiprock and never left. Every boy needs a loyal dog like Spotty, and every Spotty needs a little boy like Perry to love him.

Nita, on the other hand, loved them all. Will Rogers said that he never met a man he didn't like; Nita never saw a dog that she didn't love. This attraction was complicated by the fact that there was no animal control in Shiprock. Most Navajo families had several dogs, but when those dogs had puppies they quickly became overpopulated. Solution? Drive the puppies up to the First Baptist Church at night and put them in the yard. It didn't take long before we had far too many dogs, each one precious to Nita.

Then progress came to the reservation—an animal control shelter and officer were added to the Navajo Police Force. Of course our children, ages two, five, and seven when we moved to Shiprock, had never known about many things we as adults took for granted, such as animal control. Growing up on a reservation gave them an entirely different set of experiences.

One day Nita found Lumpy at school and brought him home wrapped in her jacket. He was without doubt the ugliest, skinniest, *lumpiest*, most pitiful dog we had ever seen. He certainly was not a keeper. Nita played with him in the yard that afternoon, but didn't look for him before she left for school the next morning. Thinking she wasn't really very attached to the mutt, Dalton said, "Hey! We have animal control now! We'll call them to come get this poor dog." We did, and they did. The dog was nothing more than a fleeting memory. Or so we thought.

That afternoon Nita came in from school, ate her usual peanut butter sandwich, and went out to play. I honestly had forgotten all about the Lumpy incident. Quite awhile later she came back into the house, obviously confused and aggravated. "I can't find Lumpy anywhere. I'll bet the Dog Catcher got him. [*thoughtful pause*] And I don't even know what a *Dog Catcher* looks like."

We even raised two calves while we lived in Shiprock, knowing their final destinies would be in the deep freeze and frying pan. We were undecided about names for the two until our friend Eric told about Oinky, a pig who, in spite of his culinary purpose in life, had become their family pet. One day Oinky fulfilled his calling: he became bacon, ham, and sausage. Eric's family sat down that evening to a platter of succulent pork chops. All went well until one of the boys looked at the platter, shook his head sadly, and began sobbing, "Poor Oinky." None of the family could finish their meal. After hearing that story, we named our two calves Steak & Hamburger.

What in the world, you are probably asking, *does all this have to do with being (or not being) a supermom?* Nothing, really, because supermoms would, I am sure, ride horses with their children, let their daughters keep lumpy puppies, and *never* plant cucumbers and cantaloupe next to one another. But in reality, most mothers are just living life one day at a time, making mistakes, doing the best they can, and allowing their children to grow up with childhood memories that time can't take away.

In the everyday lives that we spend with our young families, we are planting a garden in which will grow memories, values, discipline—those qualities upon which life should be built. I cherish my own childhood farm memories, and even though I had no desire to go back to farm life, those experiences helped me create new ones customized for my children. They probably, as city-dwelling adults, will never again have horses or raise their own Steaks and Hamburgers. But they surely do enjoy telling and re-telling those stories. My grand-children still laugh when they picture Nita riding Sugar Babe to school. Hearing Rhonda tell about holding Lester, our Lhasa Apso, while he died can bring tears to anyone's eyes. (He was named Lester because when we got him as a pup there was less "ter" him than there was "ter" most dogs.)

Dan asked me to edit a paper he had written about his and Linda's seminary years. In it he made this statement: "We thought we were getting ready to live life. We didn't realize we were living it." We didn't know when I decided to plant that garden, or when Dalton bought those horses, or when we let Perry keep Spotty and Nita watch the birth of Cockle Burr's kittens that we were giving them memories that would last a lifetime. These experiences taught them a lot about life and death and responsibility—lessons they might not have learned otherwise.

GOD'S GARDEN

Dennis Swanberg, humorist and self-proclaimed "minister of encouragement," talks about planting shade trees. The idea is that we must plant shade trees that we probably will never sit beneath. We plant them for those who follow us, for future generations. We don't have to be supermoms, but we have to plant shade trees, or at least gardens, for the gener-ations to come. When we plant the Word of God in their lives, it will grow with them, serving as a lamp to their feet and a light to their paths (Psalm 119:105). By aligning our lives with the teachings of Christ, we give them roots on which they can build their own lives.

Janet and her five-year-old daughter were making cook-ies together. Shanna looked lovingly into her mother's eyes and asked, "When I grow up, will I be like you?" That is the best kind of gardening.

What a beautiful picture of a gardener we have in John 15:1–8. God is the gardener; Jesus is the vine; we are the branches. There is so much in these verses about our relationship with our Father—the need to prune the branches so they can bear more and better fruit, the inability of the branch to bear fruit apart from the vine, the blessed life that we have when we remain connected to the life-giving vine. What a wonderful partnership we mothers can have with God the Gardener as we graft our children's lives onto the Vine.

Even Paul wrote about fruit—the fruit produced by the Holy Spirit as He lives in us (Galatians 5:22–23). Each of these characteristics or fruit can and should find complete expression in the mother role. Take *love* for instance.

Mothers are supposed to, and usually do, feel an overwhelming love when they hold their newborn baby. That love continues, even when the child is grown and perhaps no longer living. We communicate love in so many ways—through our actions, our words, our body language. Even when they are unlovely, even when they break our hearts, even when they reject our love—we still love them. As the little boy says in the commercial, mothers are like that.

PERFECT LOVE

We must always be alert to the possibility that we are communicating conditional love. Though we may not mean to, do we sometimes convey the message that "I'll love you *if* you play the sports I want you to play" or "I'll love you *when* you clean your room"? We may even let conditional love become leverage with our children. Our between-the-lines message may be that "I love your sister *because* she made *A*s on her report card; I'll love you *if* you do the same."

Pretending you've never read them before, think about

Paul's words in 1 Corinthians 13, often called the Love Chapter, and think of your role as a mother while you read. "Love never gives up. Love cares more for others than for self. Love doesn't want what it doesn't have. Love doesn't strut, doesn't have a swelled head, doesn't force itself on others, isn't always 'me first,' doesn't fly off the handle, doesn't keep score of the sins of others, doesn't revel when others grovel, takes pleasure in the flowering of truth, puts up with anything, trusts God always, always looks for the best, never looks back, but keeps going to the end" (1 Corinthians 13:4–7 *The Message*). Don't we all want love to flourish in our gardens?

JOY AND PEACE

Then there is joy. I read somewhere that joy is peace dancing; peace is joy resting. Joy—happiness—comes from an attitude of gratitude. Look for the beautiful things in life. Remember the song "Don't Worry, Be Happy"? It's not always that easy to be joyful. The realities of life can become so real and so heavy that we lose the joy of living. Mothers, if you've lost it, discover joy again. Laugh with your children. Play ball or cars or blocks with them. Build snowmen instead of complaining because it snowed. Tickle your grandchildren. Do something fun with your adult daughter. Take your daughter-in-law to her favorite place for lunch. Work a jigsaw puzzle or play a game of Chinese checkers with your son-in-law. Laugh. Don't worry. Be happy.

Peace—what a beautiful word for a mother's heart. In a later chapter you will meet my mother; she fought a 14-year battle with bone cancer. In spite of her constant pain, she knew peace. Peace is not the absence of conflict; peace is what you discover in the midst of conflict. What a beautiful thought.

Several years ago I was writing a series of articles about

"The Fruit of the Spirit and Parenting" for a parents' magazine. The very week that I was completing my article about peace I encountered one of the most difficult experiences in all of my years as a mother. As Rhonda was leaving work one evening, a man jumped into her car, held a knife to her throat, made her drive several miles from town, and raped her.

A couple of days later, after the whirl of investigations, anguish, tears, and all sorts of negative emotions, I found myself at home alone, with some time to write. *Peace?* I thought. There was no peace; in fact, there was total absence of peace. How could I ever again write about or experience peace?

I built a fire in the fireplace and sat down with a cup of coffee. Suddenly, I was totally filled with the most awesome peace I had ever known. It was as though someone had given me a pain shot and I could feel the warm medication flowing through my veins. Yet I had not taken so much as an aspirin. For about an hour I sat motionless, completely wrapped up and filled with a "peace that passeth understanding." Then I physically felt the peace leave my body; but it was okay. I knew that I must experience the agony, anger, and sadness, but I also knew that God was Peace even when we were living through that terrible storm.

And then I could write my article.

PATIENCE

How about patience? We laugh about the prayer, "Lord I need patience, and I need it right now!" We all identify; that's why we laugh. Patience while the toddler lags behind and while he learns to tie his shoe. Patience while the first grader reads a story to you. Patience when waiting for the doctor to call with the diagnosis. Patience with the teenager who knows so much more than you; patience while watching our adult child live out the consequences of some bad decisions.

Paul Harvey is famous for his "The Rest of the Story" features. His "rest of the story" reminds me that we don't know the ending to most stories we are living. Remembering that can help us patiently wait as we watch our children stumble and fall. Remembering that can help us ride out some pretty rugged storms. Remembering that can help us keep our focus on God, for He promised that "those who wait upon GOD get fresh strength. They spread their wings and soar like eagles, they run and don't get tired, they walk and don't lag behind" (Isaiah 40:31 *The Message*).

KINDNESS

Remember the verse we taught our children when they were small? "Be kind and compassionate to one another, forgiving each other, just as in Christ God forgave you" (Ephesians 4:32). I wonder how many times I used that verse to remind my children how they were to treat one another—then failed to practice it myself.

Recently I watched a mother and her two preschoolers in the grocery store. When I first saw them, the children were not misbehaving; in fact, they were doing quite well. Mother, however, was not behaving well at all. Her replies to their questions were sharp. Everything they did brought her disapproval. By the time they were ready to check out, the children were whining, clinging to her, and bothering everyone else around them.

I wanted to hold the mother's hands and say, "Be kind to them, dear one. They are little for such a short time. Listen to them. Treat them with respect." Some day I just may do that!

Goodness has been defined as coming to grips with sin and dealing with it. Goodness is its own advertisement; we don't need to tell those who are watching us whether or not we are "good." They will pick up on it quick enough! Slowing down but not stopping at a stop sign; keeping the money when the cashier gives us too much change; watching the cable TV that we haven't subscribed to; calling in sick at work when we just want the day off—such little things, but our children are watching.

They are imitating us, too. Why should we be surprised when they cheat on a test, tell a "white lie," or get a speeding ticket if we've not demonstrated goodness for them? They may still cheat and lie and speed, but if goodness was our standard, we've done our best.

FAITHFULNESS

Faithfulness—what a strong word. If I had to choose a favorite hymn it would be "Great Is Thy Faithfulness." We never say "*if* spring comes" or "*if* morning comes." We say "*when* spring comes." God is faithful. Surely, as His children, we can do no less than demonstrate faithfulness in our lives. Faithful to keep our promises—a commitment to a child is just as important (probably more important) than a promise to our employer. Faithful to pay our debts—faithful to contracts we make. John commended Gaius because "you do faithfully whatever you do" (3 John 5 NKJV). Mothers must be faithful.

Along "Motherhood Boulevard," there are some mile markers that we can go back to when we need to get our bearings on our location. I return to one of those markers that I passed on a Sunday evening. I went to church that night with a very heavy heart. One of our children was going through a difficult time. I had prayed and prayed about the situation, but there was no change and no answer. I don't think it was coincidence that one of the hymns we sang that evening was the B. B. McKinney song "Have Faith in God." The second verse was written just for me: "Have faith in God when your prayers are unanswered, your earnest plea He will never forget; wait on the Lord, trust His Word and be patient; have faith in God, He'll answer yet."

What is faith in God? Not seeing, yet we believe. Not knowing what is ahead, yet trusting Him to be there. R. A. Long was my pastor for many years, a "country preacher" whose illustrations were just right for this farm girl! He compared faith to being invited to someone's home for Sunday dinner. He said that he hoped they would have fried chicken; when he walked into the home he could smell the chicken frying. He still didn't know for sure that they would have fried chicken, but he had hope, and evidence of things not seen (see Hebrews 11:1). If we are faithful, our children will know they can trust us.

GENTLENESS AND SELF-CONTROL

Gentleness, sometimes also called meekness, is a very tasty fruit. I read somewhere that nothing is as strong as real gentleness; nothing is as gentle as real strength. Gentleness means not kicking the dog or stepping on the flowers. Gentleness is demonstrated in the way we handle dishes and comb our daughter's hair.

Mothers are supposed to have a gentle touch, right? The reality is that some people are by nature gentler than others. Think for a minute about some gentle women you have known. How did they demonstrate that gentleness? Why do you think of them this way? How can your life be gentler?

Self-control is the last in the list, and perhaps it is the most difficult. That is why we must let Christ take control. Paul said it quite well. "I tried keeping rules and working my head off to please God, and it didn't work. So I quit being a 'law man' so that I could be *God's* man. Christ's life showed me how, and enabled me to do it. I identified myself completely with him. Indeed, I have been crucified with Christ. My ego is no longer central. It is no longer important that I appear righteous before you or have your good opinion, and I am no longer driven to impress God. Christ lives in me. The life you see me living is not 'mine,' but it is lived by faith in the Son of God, who loved me and gave himself for me" (Galatians 2:19–20 *The Message*).

Self-control means saying *no* to yet another job when our plates are already too full. Self-control means saying *no* to the new furniture when we know we can't afford it. Self-control may mean not saying, "I told you so" or "Well, *duh*!"

One of my seminary professors says that what we are full of is what we will spill over when we are bumped. Mothers get bumped all the time, every day. If we are full of anger, bitterness, frustration, disappointment, or stress-controlled thoughts, that is what we will spill over onto others. But if we are filled with these characteristics of His spirit, we will spill over love, joy, peace, patience, kindness, goodness, faithfulness, gentleness, and self-control.

"Mary, Mary, quite contrary, how does your garden grow?"

"With silver bells, and cockle shells, and pretty maids all in a row."

Supermoms? No, we are just gardens producing His fruit. Tell me, how does your garden grow?

CHAPTER FIVE

Supermoms

INVEST IN REAL ESTATE

The Proverbs 31 woman not only planted a garden, or shade trees if you prefer; she bought the land on which the garden was planted. Read verse 16 again: "She looks over a field and *buys it*, then, with money she's put aside, plants a garden" (*The Message*). The Amplified Bible adds yet another thought: "She considers a [new] field before she buys or accepts it [expanding prudently and not courting neglect of her present duties by assuming other duties]." Also, "She knows when to buy or sell" (verse 18a CEV). This woman can make decisions, then act on them with wisdom and efficiency, dealing intelligently with the consequences of those decisions.

Decision Making 101 is one of those required courses in the curriculum of life, one from which we never graduate. We all make dozens of decisions daily. Some are relatively easy to make; some are extremely difficult. Some are fun; some tear our hearts out. Many are neither right nor wrong, black nor white, good nor bad. Your decision about what you wear today or what you cook for dinner will not radically change the course of history. But often many seemingly-inconsequential decisions turn out to be important.

I once heard about the CEO of a large company who suddenly resigned. His reason? Each day, all day long, he had to make many difficult decisions. He gave up his desk, computers, cell phones, and all the amenities of his position to take a menial job in the shipping department. His assignment was to sort outgoing packages according to zip codes. You guessed it! After just a few weeks he quit that job also. "Every time I picked up a package I had to make another decision," he explained.

When a friend and I met for lunch, she told me that all morning she had been making decisions—planning a meeting, completing her budget request for the coming year, interviewing a prospective employee. When the waitress brought our menu, my friend stared at it for a minute then said, "Please order for me! I cannot make one more decision!"

Usually those major decisions we must make have no precedents that we can follow, no "Decision Making for Dummies" books to give us direction. We have to use our best sense and rely on our past experiences. We sometimes have limited foreknowledge of the expected results of our decisions and how they will affect us. Often we call on others for advice. And of course, one of the best places to go is to God's advice book, commonly known as the Bible.

The psalmist tells us, "Do what the LORD wants, and he will give you your heart's desire. Let the LORD lead you and trust him to help. Then it will be as clear as the noonday sun that you were right" (Psalm 37:4–6 CEV).

The writer of Proverbs advised, "With all your heart you must trust the LORD and not your own judgment. Always let him lead you, and he will clear the road for you to follow" (Proverbs 3:5–6 CEV).

TIPS FOR DECIDING

While every decision is unique, basic problem-solving techniques can be used in most situations. I'm certainly no expert in either problem-solving or decision-making, but I have discovered some helpful steps.

The first thing to do is identify the problem or decision to be made. Give it a name. Write a one-sentence description. Often this simple step helps me get a handle on what I'm facing. Monsters with names are easier to conquer than nameless ones. On occasion I've even realized when naming the problem that the real problem was not at all what I thought it was.

Next, identify the source. Ask yourself questions such as, *Why is it a problem? Why is the decision a difficult one? What are the obvious factors and causes? The not-so-obvious ones?*

There are other factors to consider. Is there a time frame for handling the problem or making the decision? What will be the impact on your life and on the lives of others? What are your motives for the decision you make? Write possible solutions or alternatives, even ones that you know aren't possible or feasible. Now mark them as desirable or undesirable, then rank them according to the best solution or decision. Ask others for advice if appropriate. Look to others who have had the same or similar problem. What did they do? Was it good or bad? Would it work for you or not?

As you think of solutions, mentally or on paper follow through with the consequences of those solutions. Obviously, you cannot predict every outcome; you can't know the future. But there are some end results that are relatively certain.

And *pray.* Before you do any of the actions above, pray. Ask for wisdom. James had quite a bit to say about this very subject. "Consider it a sheer gift, friends, when tests and challenges come at you from all sides. You know that under pressure, your faith-life is forced into the open and shows its true colors. So don't try to get out of anything prematurely. Let it do its work so you become mature and well-developed, not deficient in any way. If you don't know what you're doing, pray to the Father. He loves to help. You'll get his help, and won't be condescended to when you ask for it. Ask boldly, believingly, without a second thought. People who 'worry their prayers' are like wind-whipped waves" (James 1:2–6 *The Message*).

MAKE YOUR MOVE

After we've prayed and weighed all our options, there comes a time when we must make our move. After the Israelites left Egypt, they wandered forty years in the desert. But in God's timing, when they were ready to claim the Promised Land, God told the people it was time to quit praying and move. There is a time to pray and a time to move.

Shortly before Joshua died he gathered the people of Israel together and gave them some advice about a very important decision. His words can also help us as we make many of our decisions. "Choose for yourselves this day whom you will serve, whether the gods which your fathers served that were on the other side of the River, or the gods of the Amorites, in whose land you dwell. But as for me and my house, we will serve the LORD" (Joshua 24:15 NKJV). Is my decision going to honor the Lord? Will it help my family see that He is the Lord of my life?

Back to our friend Miriam—she looked at the land, then made a decision. She followed through and came up with the cash. Surely she had some decisions to make before making her purchase. Would the land meet her needs? Was it worth the asking price? Did she have the money to buy it or would she have to take out a loan? She probably considered the consequences, too. Would she be the one to farm it? Or would she lease it, or perhaps sell it for a profit? Who else would be affected by her decision?

The Amplified Bible brings up another question: how would her decision affect her other responsibilities and duties? Some decisions must be made based on the absolute realities of life. Sometimes we just have to admit that we don't have the time, the money, or other resources to make the decision we might like to make. When all three of our children were still at home we made a job change, which meant a move. In looking for a temporary place to live, the realtor showed us a beautiful home with a swimming pool. The problems were that it was only for sale, not rent or lease; it was very expensive; and our previous house had not yet sold. Buying the new home was completely out of the question for the adults, but we surely got a lot of pressure from three would-be swimmers to buy it anyway. They even offered to give up their allowances if that would help!

Junior the dog had been a part of Rhonda's pet family since his birth. When the veterinarian discovered a large mass in his intestines, they had three choices: expensive, painful surgery that might not help; putting him to sleep; giving him pain medication as he lived out his last days at home. Surgery was out because of the cost and uncertainty of the outcome. Rhonda's husband had recently put one dog to sleep, and could not bear to do that to fourteen-year-old Junior. They chose to keep him medicated with morphine until his death. Just a dog? Yes, but a good example of a difficult decision. I'm sure you understand if you've ever had a dog who was part of your family.

THE MENDING TABLE APPROACH

Of course sometimes I want to take the mending table approach to making decisions. When my children were small I enjoyed making most of their clothes, but I hated to mend. I would put a shirt that needed a button or a jacket with a broken zipper on my sewing table, with honest intentions of mending it. But I just kept putting off the task I didn't want to do. One day I realized that if I left the mending there long enough, the child would outgrow the item to be mended. Oh, well—might as well give it away.

Most decisions can't be left on the mending table until they are irrelevant or the crisis is past. How do you deal with a child who is in trouble with the law? How do you make life-and-death medical decisions? How do you solve financial crises? Working mothers have a unique set of childcare decisions to make. What do you do on days when there's no school or the child is sick, but mom still has to work? What about those two hours after school before mom or dad come home?

I am thinking of two mothers who even as I write this are facing some monumental decisions and the results of those decisions. Nancy learned that her teenaged son sexually molested a neighbor girl; she made the decision to turn him over to the authorities. Lois must decide for or against surgery for her physically handicapped son. Without the surgery he will spend the rest of his life in a wheelchair. Yet the surgery will be extremely painful and pose a great risk to his life with only a 40% percent chance of success.

We begin making decisions for and about our children even before they are born. The pregnant mother decides which foods she will eat and what vitamins she will take to nurture the little one forming inside her. Do I learn the unborn baby's sex or not? Then the decisions gradually become more complicated. Do I breastfeed or use formula? Decisions arise about daycare, baby-sitters, potty training, and which brand of peanut butter to buy. How do I deal with temper tantrums? With picky eaters? With a bed wetter? Which schools will they attend, or shall I homeschool? When do I let her date? Should my high school student get a job or play basketball? Is it better that he take a car to college, or that he depend on friends to drive him?

A bit overwhelming, isn't it? As I write this, I ask myself, *Why would anyone want to be a mother? Why would we want to subject ourselves to all these decisions that come with the job?* And I answer myself, *Because motherhood is the greatest job I know of!* We often make the wrong decisions; we can't solve many of the problems we encounter. But once in awhile, when we least expect it, we come through with flying colors. We say no, and months—or perhaps years—later, our children say, "Thank you for saying no that time." My Rhonda recently told me about her decision not to let one of her daughters do what the daughter wanted to do. Rhonda said, "She wasn't happy with me, so I must have made the right decision."

In a later chapter we will talk about the supermom's desire to control the actions, thoughts, and destinies of her children. Many of the decisions we make are based on our attempt to guide others. That is neither a totally bad nor good thing. We are supposed to bring up our children "in the way they should go." At the same time, we must equip them to make their own decisions. They need to learn that there are negative consequences to some decisions and positive outcomes to others. If you touch a hot stove, it will burn you.

They also need to know that many times they are given second chances, but often they must also live with some of the consequences. I have heard it said that God can remove the nail, but often God does not remove the nail hole. It is still there, reminding us of the nail that was once there.

As our children grow older, though, we need to reassure them of God's promise that "If we confess our sins, He is faithful and just to forgive us our sins and to cleanse us from all unrighteousness" (1 John 1:9 NKJV). An unwed mother-to-be told me she was convinced that God could not forgive her sin. As I read this verse to her I continued, "...cleanse us from all unrighteousness except having sex before marriage." She suddenly realized the huge expanse of that little word *all*. She had the baby, and the rest of her life was changed because of the consequences of her sin. But life went on, and she became a good mother, a forgiven child of God.

TOUGH DECISIONS

While Perry was in high school we attended a family camp. One evening at the close of the worship service, Perry told one of the counselors God was calling him to some kind of full-time Christian service. Later, as he and I walked back to our cabin, he said, "But Mama, I don't know *what* God wants me to do." As we talked, I thought of an illustration. I have used this many times since with other young people wondering about their futures.

"When you're driving at night you turn on your headlights. You can see only so far ahead of you. That's okay, because you know that as you move forward you will see even further ahead. You still won't see the end of the road, but you can see just far enough to allow you to move ahead. If you stop, afraid of the darkness beyond the limits of your lights, you will never see any further than what you can see right now. But if you keep moving ahead in the light that you have, you will continue to see more and more."

I have not only used the headlight illustration with young people; I have reminded myself of it on several occasions. Sometimes, in my attempts to be supermom, I forget that I don't have to be all-knowing. I want to shine a spotlight into the darkness, revealing some of the hidden dangers lurking ahead. Other times I don't even want to move, and I'm paralyzed by the fear of what might be hiding in the dark.

During the time I was writing this chapter, I spent a few days at a retreat with a group of women. Joanne (names have been changed) had just learned that her adult daughter was an alcoholic, and was struggling with her role in this unrehearsed life drama. Diane had after much prayer and conversation finally told her high school senior that she could fly 600 miles to spend her spring break with her college boyfriend. Serena was facing an entirely new set of decisions as she became "mother" to her own mother. And Donna asked us to pray for her friends whose son had run into a tree while skiing, and was now in a coma. Doctors had told the parents they might soon have to decide whether or not to take him off life support.

So Supermom buys some land, then plants a garden on it. The psalmist summed up this and the previous chapter quite well when he wrote, "you thrill to God's Word, you chew on Scripture day and night. You're a tree replanted in Eden, bearing fresh fruit every month, never dropping a leaf, always in blossom....God charts the road you take" (Psalm 1:2–3, 6a *The Message*).

Make wise, God-guided decisions that will allow you to plant trees on them—decisions you and others can live with. Decisions that will be profitable and productive. And may your investments be profitable and your garden flourish.

CHAPTER SIX

Supermoms
COMPETE IN
MRS. AMERICA PAGEANTS

She may not be declared the winner, but a true supermom would surely be one of the runners-up, don't you think? Just picture her, gliding gracefully across the stage, giving the beauty-queen wave to her adoring audience. She designed and sewed her evening gown; her hair is perfectly coiffed; her makeup is applied so well that no one would ever be able to guess her age. She even looked great in her swimsuit just a few minutes before making her walk of fame.

Judges in beauty contests consider many areas of the contestants' lives when making their decisions—appearance, talent, physical fitness, and so forth. I'm not sure beauty contests were around when Proverbs 31 was written (in fact, I seriously doubt that they were), but had they been I do believe our Miriam would have won first place. Just look at her credentials:

- "She makes her own clothing, and dresses in colorful linens and silks" (verse 22 *The Message*).

- "Her clothing is of linen, pure and fine, and of purple [such as that of which the clothing of the priests and the hallowed clothes of the temple are made]" (verse 22 AMP).
- "She does her own sewing, and everything she wears is beautiful" (verse 22 CEV).
- "Her clothes are well-made and elegant" (verse 25a *The Message*).
- "She is strong and graceful" (verse 25a CEV).

Not only are her looks impeccable, while she might not work out at the gym every morning, she was certainly a specimen of physical fitness.

- "She girds herself with strength [spiritual, mental, and physical fitness for her God-given task] and makes her arms strong and firm" (verse 17 AMP).
- "She girds herself with strength, and strengthens her arms" (verse 17 NKJV).

So how can we 21st century mothers—wearing faded jeans and no makeup, with split ends in our graying hair, and 20 pounds overweight—relate to this supermom? Do we have a chance? What if we don't exercise five days a week? What if we weigh too much or not enough? What fitness guru sets the standard for that, anyway? Let's have a little contest of our own and see how we rate.

Look at what we are told about our friend Miriam. She made her clothes; they were made from fine fabric and obviously appropriate for her. Now look at what we are not told about her. She may not have been especially beautiful as the world judges beauty. Perhaps her feet or nose were too big, or she was too short or too tall.

So often what we dislike most about ourselves are those things that we can do nothing to change. We ask, "Mirror, mirror on the wall, who's the fairest of them all?" knowing that we certainly won't qualify. We can't see beyond our wrinkles, unruly hair, and freckles. Even with all its faults, think about what a marvelous body you have. Instead of focusing on what's *wrong* with our bodies, we should think about what's *right,* what God has blessed us with. Starting with your head and working your way down to your feet, thank God for all those parts that make up your body. Some are tiny; some are large (or at least larger than we wish they were). But all of them together form a temple that God gave you, a vehicle to help you travel through this world. Supermoms may have perfect, glamorous bodies, but aren't you thankful for the body God gave you?

I am sad when I see a mother who doesn't take care of her appearance. Joye buys most of her clothes at a thrift store, but she always looks fabulous. Another woman, however, buys her clothes at a moderately expensive dress shop, but often when I see her she looks unkempt. We don't have to spend a lot of money on clothes, jewelry, and makeup to look our best. Be yourself. Some women enjoy wearing a lot of jewelry; some wear little or none. Some take 30 minutes every morning to put on their make-up; others hurriedly apply a little lipstick. We just need to be proud of who we are. After all, we are daughters of the King!

FINDING YOUR STYLE

I worked for several years with a woman who always looked magnificent. She often wore silk dresses with pleated skirts, and every one of her beautiful silver hairs was always in place. We sometimes joked that "casual" for her meant one strand of pearls! Another coworker usually wore denim jumpers, or if she really dressed up, she probably had on a pantsuit. Hooray for both of them! They both found the style that fit them best.

In my early motherhood years, I weighed between 110 and 115 pounds. One day I was driving to the store with five-year-old Perry in the back seat and seven-year-old Rhonda in the front beside me. Nothing had been said for several blocks when Perry leaned forward against the front seat (that was before seat-belt days), sighed, and said sadly, "It's okay. I don't care if I have a fat mama." I have no idea where he had heard that or why he said it, but it certainly made an impression on me! I'm not sure what that has to do with being a supermom, or winning beauty contests, or dressing well. Perhaps it is just a reminder that no matter how we see ourselves, there is usually someone there to keep our feet planted firmly on the ground!

Now let's see how we rate on the physical fitness scale. I know that exercise is important; I just don't do it like I should. At night I put a block of wood on the floor and run around it twice so I can say I jogged around the block a couple of times. I did buy myself a treadmill; it works very well as a place to hang clothes that are to be ironed.

Betty, who is a nurse, says that there's no way we can do everything we are supposed to do each evening—exercise, cleanse our face, read the Bible, take our vitamins, and floss our teeth, to name just a few. She has given me some advice that I try to follow. When she goes to the grocery store, she parks at the back of the lot so she will get exercise as she walks to the store. The store where she shops still has sack boys who carry out groceries. As they walk across the parking lot, she talks with him about her relationship with Christ. Betty also says that if your husband really loves you, he'll park a long distance from the store so you will have to walk. She adds, "Sometimes I wish he didn't love me quite so much!"

A few years ago a vitamin advertisement said that a healthy woman "eats right, gets plenty of rest, and takes Geritol." It is important that we eat the right foods. As much as I love them, I don't need potato chips with my sandwich. A cup of lowfat yogurt is a much healthier snack than a bowl of ice cream. Do you really need that second helping? How about ordering a grilled chicken salad instead of a hamburger when you are at a fast-food restaurant? A supermom might be a health food nut but every woman should be wise about the foods she eats.

Our bodies, imperfections and all, are a gift from God. We should treat them as such and prize them highly. While Dalton spent one year as an army chaplain in Vietnam, I went to college full-time, served in several leadership positions in my church, and organized a support group for other "waiting wives." (That was before we were called a "support group.") In addition, I was trying to be both mama and daddy to three children. My usual breakfast? A Dr. Pepper and a donut. My usual lunch? A Dr. Pepper, some chips, and maybe a sandwich. My usual dinner? A Dr. Pepper along with whatever I fixed for Rhonda, Perry, and Nita.

After several months of this unhealthy routine, I had some major physical problems. While trying to be supermom, I failed to use my common sense. After running several tests, the doctor found that my body was totally deficient in niacin. My wake-up call taught me how important it is that I take care of myself. And that was one more mile marker on my road to *not* being a supermom!

You've probably heard about the man and woman who died and were exclaiming over the beauties of heaven. The husband remarked to his wife, "And just think—we'd have been here five years sooner if you hadn't made us eat all that oat bran."

We also need to take care of our bodies in other ways. Do you have yearly mammograms and exams? My mother died many years ago from breast cancer. I've often wondered if I would have had her longer had she had the opportunity to have exams as we do now. Do you watch your cholesterol count? Do you take a calcium supplement?

One of my cousins had been having some health problems, but the doctor couldn't seem to find what was wrong. His mother, a professional worrier, was sure that some powerful vitamins would help. The next time I saw my cousin he said the doctor had given him a vitamin B shot. "Did it help you?" I asked.

"No," he replied, "but it sure made Mama feel a lot better."

No physical body is perfect. Just like personalities, each is unique. Why not celebrate the differences instead of crying about them? I had been in Patti's home a number of times before I realized there was something very unusual about the way she folded her laundry and peeled potatoes. I learned that she was born with a healthy left arm and only a stump where her right arm should have been. I never heard her complain about what I saw as a limitation; just the opposite was true. She could do more with her two hands—one human and one artificial—than most people do with two human hands. She reared four boys, re-upholstered furniture, taught school, and did beautiful needlework. Come to think of it, if I could nominate someone as an authentic supermom, Patti would get my vote.

REST IS SPIRITUAL, TOO

How much rest do you get each night? Do you take time for yourself? I recall a time when I was trying to be supermom, super wife, super employee, super everything else that was on my plate. I guess my tiredness showed on my face when

I showed up for church that night, because my pastor told me something I've never forgotten. "Sometimes the most spiritual thing you can do is rest."

Miriam had to have a lot of strength and energy to do all that she did. "First thing in the morning, she dresses for work, rolls up her sleeves, eager to get started. She senses the worth of her work, is in no hurry to call it quits for the day" (verses 17–18 *The Message*). Haven't you had days when you enjoyed so much what you were doing that you just didn't want the day to end? You were energized by your involvement. Don't you wish you had more days like that?

After Mary had a stroke she told me that she was learning a difficult lesson. "I used to ask God every morning, 'What do You want me to do today?' Now I have to ask Him, 'What do You want me to *be* today?'" There are lessons to be learned when we slow down. We have time to reflect on the real priorities of life. We suddenly see the butterflies instead of the hedge that needs to be trimmed. We bless others by allowing them to help us. New leaders step forward when the need arises; others discover skills and strengths that we were not allowing them to use when we were trying to do it all ourselves.

How balanced is your life? Do you take time for yourself? Children, spouse, job, church, friends, and neighbors all demand a part of us. The supermom thinks that she must, like Paul, be all things to all people (1 Corinthians 9:22) all the time. The wise woman knows how to set priorities and to schedule time for herself. Once, after speaking at a retreat about our mission work, a woman asked me what my greatest challenge was. I'm sure she was thinking my answer would be something like cultural adjustments, or learning the Navajo language, or living on the reservation. After some thought I replied, "Saying no." I imagine most mothers feel the same way. There are so many *good* things that we could and should do. If you have the same problem I do, you might want to spend some time in front of the mirror practicing saying that hard-to-pronounce word: no, no, no.

The woman who is really effective is the one who does the job God has given her, not the jobs the world tries to give her. Remember what the Amplified Bible said about the land Miriam bought? "Expanding prudently and not courting neglect of her present duties by assuming other duties" (verse 16). Sometimes, in our busyness, we are more like a raging stream racing down the mountainside than we are like a deep, calm lake. The rushing river uproots trees and tears down the banks along the sides. The woman who tries to be supermom is frustrated, unhappy, and possibly has an ulcer.

In his book *When the Aardvark Parked on the Ark*, Calvin Miller writes about the sawed-off seesaw. He says that "in life or on seesaws good balance is key. To zoom up and down and enjoy your ride be sure that your board is the same on both sides." Would you describe your board as the same on both sides, your life as well-rounded? (No, I'm not talking about your body now! Perhaps you, like me, can relate to the man who said, "I'm in shape. Round is a shape.") I would describe Miriam's life as well rounded, wouldn't you? Look at verse 14: "She is like the merchant ships loaded with foodstuffs; she brings her household's food from a far [country]" (AMP). Or as Peterson says in *The Message*, "She's like a trading ship that sails to faraway places and brings back exotic surprises." She surely had a flair for the unusual, the spontaneous, sometimes even the outrageous.

YOU'RE AN INDIVIDUAL

Celebrate your uniqueness as an individual. You don't have to be like anyone else, you know. Be the very best possible *you*.

Capitalize on your strengths; minimize your weaknesses; accept your limitations. A little boy was watching a spider at work. Turning to his father, he said, "Gee, Dad, I am so much smarter than that spider. I can talk, think, read, and do things a spider can never do."

The wise father replied, "Yes, you are right. But can you spin a web?"

I've always liked the story about the little boy playing outside the kitchen window. Mother watched as Johnny threw the baseball up into the air and declared, "I'm the world's greatest batter!" He missed. Again he threw the ball into the air, and again declared, "I'm the world's greatest batter!" as he swung and missed. This happened several more times, and mother was beginning to worry about Johnny's self-image. No problem, however. A few minutes later she watched as he threw, swung, missed, and declared, "I'm the world's greatest pitcher!"

Supermom thinks she has to do everything, and do it perfectly. You and I know that's impossible. My grandmother used to tell me, "If a task is once begun, never leave it till it's done. Be the labor great or small, do it well or not at all." That advice is partially good, but not completely. We should do our best, true, but sometimes we also need to remember Richard Carlson's advice in his book *Don't Sweat the Small Stuff...and It's All Small Stuff*. He says, "I've yet to meet an absolute perfectionist whose life was filled with inner peace. The need for perfection and the desire for inner tranquility conflict with each other."

Develop those abilities that are uniquely yours. Get that degree you've always wanted; take piano or drawing lessons; join that choir or orchestra. Don't worry if you don't become a Vladimir Horowitz or Van Gogh. I drew a tree for one of my grandchildren. Her older sister looked at it and advised, "Nana, I think you'd better stick to writing."

We can have pity parties with almost any theme. I know—I've had plenty of them. There's the "I wish I were younger" party, and the "My husband doesn't send me flowers" party. The woman who has a job but no children feels sorry for herself; the mother who has children but no job feels sorry for herself because she has to stay at home; the mother who has children and a job feels sorry for herself because she has to work. At times we all need to count our blessings and read again Paul's words to the church at Philippi: "I've learned by now to be quite content whatever my circumstances. I'm just as happy with little as with much, with much as with little. I've found the recipe for being happy whether full or hungry, hands full or hands empty. Whatever I have, wherever I am, I can make it through anything in the One who makes me who I am" (Philippians 4:11–13 *The Message*).

Do you love yourself? That is a command, you know. On several occasions Jesus told His followers they were to "love others as well as you love yourself" (Matthew 22:39 *The Message*). We usually focus so much on loving others that we forget we are also to love ourselves. You're a special person, you know. You're made in your Father's image.

Recently I was looking through some of my journals and found this entry:

> The conference was *so* inspiring—on being a woman who is "altogether lovely." I went home and stood looking into the mirror. A few gray hairs, a few extra pounds, a pair of pants I've worn for three years, an oversized sweat shirt with a stain on one cuff, and a pair of tennis shoes that don't match my pants. What shall I do? I *must* do something! I don't look "altogether lovely"; I don't feel "altogether lovely."

So I had a Mary Kay facial; I had a manicure—and a pedicure too! I bought myself a new watch and a gold ring. I had my hair styled in the latest fashion and had my teeth polished pearly white. I did aerobics twice a week and took vitamins every day. I took a course in how to walk, how to talk, how to sit, what to say. I put on a Liz Claiborne skirt with a Gloria Vanderbilt blouse. I carried a Gucci bag and wore Via Spiga shoes.

Then I stood looking into the mirror. Ah, yes! Surely *now* I am altogether lovely! So I had my picture made and put it into my family album. Right next to a picture of my mama, wearing a dress she made from a chicken feed sack. She had on no makeup. Her hair was in a knot at the back of her head. It must have been time for her twice-a-year trip to the beauty shop for a perm. Her hands were rough; her nails were chipped from working in the field.

But in her eyes—oh, what love! Wait a minute! My mother is altogether lovely. Have I missed the point? Not completely. *Altogether* lovely means inside *and* outside. The wrapping on a package is important; that makes people want to open the box and see what's inside. But the inside must be lovely, too.

Someone said that God's good gifts often come to us wrapped in people. If I am to be one of God's good gifts to others, I need to work on being *altogether* lovely. The wrapping should be neat and lovely. The contents should be lovely, too.

Lord, help me to be altogether lovely so that I may be an effective reflection of You.

You've probably seen the poem that declares, "When I am an old woman, I shall wear purple." I've decided I'm going to wear purple now. I am going to be a deep, calm lake, not a raging stream. I'm going to take Paul's admonition to "Take your everyday, ordinary life—your sleeping, eating, going-to-work, and walking-around life—and place it before God as an offering. Embracing what God does for you is the best thing you can do for him. Don't become so well-adjusted to your culture that you fit into it without even thinking. Instead, fix your attention on God. You'll be changed from the inside out. Readily recognize what he wants from you, and quickly respond to it. Unlike the culture around you, always dragging you down to its level of immaturity, God brings the best out of you, develops well-formed maturity in you" (Romans 12:1–2 *The Message*).

You know what? I think I'll just let the supermoms go through all that agony trying to win the Mrs. America pageants. I'm going to go shopping for a new dress!

CHAPTER SEVEN

Supermoms

DON'T DIE

That thought kept ringing in my mind as I watched the father and his two young daughters. Not more than ten feet in front of them sat a silver box made of cold metal. Some call it a casket; Savannah called it Mama's velvet bed. *Supermoms don't die*, my mind cried out again. But the reality is they do. This 28-year-old mother just happened to be in the wrong place at the wrong time—and a fiery automobile crash took her life.

The truth is, mothers of all ages die. My friend Karen lost her battle with ovarian cancer when her daughter was 12 years old. Claude's 18-year-old mother died giving birth to her first son. My grandmother was 98 when we told her goodbye for the last time. My father, her 80-year-old son, said, "You'd think that after 98 years we'd be ready to give her up, but we just had that many more years to get used to having her with us." To him, she was still Mom.

I have now celebrated more birthdays than did my mother. In the fall of her 44th year she made that terrifying discovery that so many women have made—a lump in her right breast.

Knowing what the diagnosis would be, Mama kept her secret for several weeks before she even told my daddy. In the surgical waiting room after performing a radical mastectomy, the doctors told Daddy she might live six months, if we were fortunate. I began my first year in high school that fall.

Mama knew how serious her condition was, but they forgot to tell her she was only supposed to live six months. She lived the six months—and another 14 years. As it often does, the cancer moved into her bones. At times I am sure the pain must have been excruciatingly unbearable. X-rays showed ribs that looked like sponges. In some places bones not much larger than a hair were all that held her neck together. One Sunday morning, when returning to her seat after playing the piano for church, the femur of her right leg broke. She never walked again, but spent the last two years of her life in a wheelchair.

From the beginning of this chapter of her life, Mama's prayer was that God would allow her to live until I finished high school. God did allow that; she also lived long enough to know my husband Dalton, and her grandchildren Rhonda, Perry, and Nita. The children and I lived just a few blocks from my folks during the year Dalton was a military chaplain in Vietnam. Mother died knowing we would soon be commissioned as missionaries, and that I had begun my writing career. She got to share all the major events of my life up to that point. God answered her prayers in abundance.

The day she died (it was Sunday), she awakened from a coma-like sleep, held my daddy's hand, and quoted part of Jesus' precious promise in the fourteenth chapter of John. "Let not your heart be troubled: ye believe in God, believe also in me. In my Father's house are many mansions: if it were not so, I would have told you. I go to prepare a place for you. And if I go and prepare a place for you, I will come again, and receive you unto myself; that where I am, there ye may be also" (John 14:1–3 KJV). That night she spread her wings and soared with the eagles. Even more wonderful, she *walked* and was not weary, she *ran* and didn't faint (Isaiah 40:31).

Why did God allow us to have her so much longer than we were supposed to? I'm not sure, but I know that during those 14 years she taught me and others so many things about life. Still today, more than 30 years later, I meet people who tell me, "Your mother was such a blessing to me and to our church." Not long ago, after speaking in a church, a woman told me, "Your mother was my Sunday school teacher. I still remember things she taught me. I wish I could tell her that." So do I.

FREEDA'S STORY

You've heard the expression "sing like an angel"? Freeda could out-sing the angels. Her voice was clear, strong, and beautiful. Now she was in the hospital recovering from brain surgery. The doctors told her husband Coy that it would only be a matter of days before she was gone; the tumor could not be removed and it was pressing against her optic nerve.

When Coy went to visit her, she asked him to turn up the light because it was dark in the room. He had to tell her what the doctor had told him—that her vision would only get worse in the days ahead before the cancer claimed her life. Freeda lay silent for a few minutes, processing what she had just heard. Then, without a quiver in her voice, she began to sing. "When peace, like a river, attendeth my way, when sorrows like sea billows roll; whatever my lot, Thou hast taught me to say, It is well, it is well with my soul." How the words must have echoed down the hospital corridor!

Her birthday was one week later. Coy and her two sons brought a birthday cake to her room and placed it on her tray.

While they were singing "Happy Birthday" to her, Freeda went home to be with the Lord. What a birthday present for her!

No, my mother and Freeda weren't supermoms. They had faults, insecurities, fears, and disappointments just like every one else. But as mothers of every generation have done for their children and many others, they taught us how to live and how to die. The Proverbs 31 mother "doesn't worry about her family when it snows; their winter clothes are all mended and ready to wear" (verse 21 *The Message*). Every day mothers are making winter clothes for their families, preparing them for whatever storms may be ahead. Although she suffered so much, Mama was fortunate that she had years to prepare herself and her family for the winter that was coming; Freeda hardly had that chance. Most of us have no weather forecast to tell us a storm is approaching, so we need to keep the mending up to date. How do we do that? That's what the rest of this chapter is all about.

PREPARING FOR WINTER

We prepare our family and ourselves intentionally and with planning; we also prepare them while we are in the process of living every day. For one thing, we need to help our children learn that death is not something to be feared, but is a part of life. Nita was five when my mother died. A few months after Mama's funeral, Nita called me into her bedroom. "Mama, does Grandma live in our hearts?" she asked.

Not exactly sure how to answer, I said, "Well, sort of. Why?"

"Well, Grandma's gone to live with Jesus. And Jesus lives in our hearts. So doesn't Grandma live in our hearts, too?" I had to admit she had a good point! In all these years since Mama died, I think a part of her still lives in our hearts. I see her in my Rhonda. I still dream about her occasionally. I think of her often, remembering things she taught me, things she said and did, ways her life still influences my own.

As I was writing this book, my daddy, at age 91, died on December 29, four days after Christmas. (He died on Sunday, too!) We thought he was going to die on Christmas day. Kendyl, my eleven-year-old granddaughter, said, "We'll give Granddaddy to Jesus for His birthday."

It certainly seems as though death will never come to us, especially when we are young. After my daddy's death, Rhonda's daughters were talking about him, remembering times they had spent with him. Someone said something about me. Jenna quickly said, "But Nana won't ever die." I must admit I like her attitude! But the reality is, I will die, and so will everyone else if our Lord doesn't come back before then.

Perry, who is now a hospital chaplain, frequently speaks to hospice care groups. He told me about speaking to one group. His speech began with this statement: "I have a terminal disease. It was diagnosed when the doctor said, 'Congratulations, Mr. and Mrs. Edwards. You are the proud parents of a baby boy.'" Someone said that "being healthy just means that we are dying slower."

What a gift it is to be ready for death when it does come! But it is also a gift to live life to its fullest while we are alive. Not long ago, my 80-year-old neighbor died and I went to her estate sale. Her dishes, doll collection, sheets and towels, canned food, sofa pillows—everything she had owned was now being bought and carried out of the house by strangers. The room filled with fabric and quilting supplies had more of an atmosphere of a department store bargain basement than the room where she spent most of her days, carefully creating beautiful quilts.

At first I found myself becoming depressed as I watched what was happening. Then I realized that she had lived life just as she should have—enjoying every day, making memories that lived on after she was gone. If she could have been there, she would probably have enjoyed the company and all the hustle-bustle that was going on.

When we practice living by faith, living with our lives in His hands, trusting Him to lead us each day, we are more nearly ready for the storms. The winds still howl, and the rain beats around us, but we hold tight to the One who has the power to calm the storms.

I once heard an illustration about a young man hired to work on a farm. During the night a fierce storm hit. The farmer, hearing the commotion outside, ran to the young man's bedroom, only to find him sound asleep. Waking him, the farmer asked, "How can you sleep through this storm?"

The hired hand replied that he had secured the barn doors, put all the livestock in safe locations, and put all the tools inside. He could sleep through the storm because he was prepared. What a beautiful illustration of Proverbs 3:23–25: "You will walk safely and never stumble; you will rest without a worry and sleep soundly. So don't be afraid of sudden disasters or storms that strike those who are evil" (CEV), or "No need to panic over alarms or surprises, or predictions that doomsday's just around the corner, because God will be right there with you; he'll keep you safe and sound" (Proverbs 3:25–26 *The Message*).

I've known women, and I'm sure you have too, who avoided at all costs talking about death. Some refused to learn how to handle family finances as though not having that knowledge could prevent her husband's death. For some, the fear of death is so great that they even avoid making a will or any other arrangements. But for the believer, the subject of death is not morbid; it is talk about graduation time and a grand adventure.

If you were to ask the unborn baby, "Do you really want to be born?" he would probably reply, "Of course not! Why would

I want to leave the warmth and security of my mother's womb to enter a cold, harsh world?" Once the umbilical cord is cut, he's pretty much on his own. He now has to breathe and drink in order to stay alive, and he will surely need a good set of lungs in order to notify his parents when he needs something. Yet we know that it is much better to be an independent person than a dependent fetus.

So it is with death. Some day, according to Paul, "Our dead and decaying bodies will be changed into bodies that won't die or decay. The bodies we now have are weak and can die. But they will be changed into bodies that are eternal. Then the Scriptures will come true, 'Death has lost the battle! Where is its victory? Where is its sting?'" (1 Corinthians 15:53–55 CEV). And John adds, "He will wipe all tears from their eyes, and there will be no more death, suffering, crying, or pain. These things of the past are gone forever" (Revelation 21:4 CEV).

Paul wasn't afraid to die. In fact, he said that "If I live, it will be for Christ, and if I die, I will gain even more. I don't know what to choose. I could keep on living and doing something useful. It is a hard choice to make. I want to die and be with Christ, because that would be much better" (Philippians 1:21–23 CEV). Just think—in heaven there will be no rebellion, no sin, no temptations, no words we wish we could recall, no impossible decisions to make, no need to be supermom. There will just be victory!

SEWING FOR THE FUTURE

I find it interesting that so many verses in Proverbs 31 refer to sewing. Sewing is scriptural, you know— "As you sew, so shall ye rip." God even made clothes for Adam and Eve after their sin. He killed one of His creatures in order to make a covering for the guilty couple. He still covers us today through the death of His own dear Son. The verse we've already mentioned in this chapter (Proverbs 31:21) says that her winter clothes are all mended, ready for the snow. Look at some of the other verses that refer to sewing:

- "With her own hands she gladly makes clothes" (verse 13 CEV).
- "She spins her own cloth" (verse 19 CEV).
- "She does her own sewing, and everything she wears is beautiful" (verse 22 CEV).
- "She makes clothes to sell to the shop owners" (verse 24 CEV).
- "She shops around for the best yarns and cottons, and enjoys knitting and sewing" (verse 13 *The Message*).
- "She designs gowns and sells them, brings the sweaters she knits to the dress shops. Her clothes are well-made and elegant" (verses 24–25a *The Message*). Then verse 25 adds, "and she always faces tomorrow with a smile" (*The Message*), or she is "cheerful about the future" (CEV).

I think there is a connection here. Think of the kinds of "clothes" that mothers are to sew for their families—clothes of prayer, faith, trust, confidence, focus, purpose. Clothes to keep them warm; clothes to protect them from the elements; clothes that complement them and make them attractive.

Remember that Miriam did not have a Wal-Mart or Sears just down the street. Making clothes and even the fabric from which they were cut was an essential part of her life. So often we find that we must do those things that are essential, even if they aren't our favorite thing to do.

Soon after Rhonda married, she had a blood clot in her lungs, a result of the birth control pills she was taking. Her doctor took her off the pill and started her on Coumaden, a blood thinner. Of course she got pregnant. Because she could not stop taking a blood thinner, but Coumaden could cause birth defects, every 12 hours she had to give herself a Heparin shot, another blood thinner, in the stomach. A friend asked her, "How can you do that?"

She replied, "You just do what you have to do."

What do we do when we mend clothes? We are just doing what has to be done. We look for rips and tears, replace lost buttons, tack loose hems. When we sense a "rip" in our children's lives, we need to be ready with materials to make a patch, or at least to offer materials so they can sew the patch. I've already confessed my dislike for mending, but the fact remains that if I'm going to wear the dress again, it must be mended.

CLOTHES FOR THE SEASONS

Taking an inventory of our children's clothes as they grow is an ongoing process. I remember picking up a favorite shirt or dress that had been outgrown and sadly putting it in the give-away box. As summer ended, I would look through their closets to see what school clothes they would need. We need to inventory other areas of their lives, too. Have they outgrown some of the things we taught them as little children? Are they ready for new lessons, new horizons? Are there spiritual, emotional, developmental clothes they are going to need as they go out into a cold world?

We are not only sewing warm clothes for our children; we are building an ark for them. We are teaching them that there is a place of security where they can go when it seems that the rains will never stop. While we are teaching them how to die, we are at the same time teaching them how to live. Our children have temptations that we never did face. They need self-confidence—need to know it's okay to say no. They need direction about choices they will make in life, so they will be able on their own to "inspect and buy a field."

We must make warm clothes for ourselves, too. When flying on an airplane, the flight attendant will tell you that if the oxygen mask drops, we should first put it on ourselves, then put one on our child. If our clothes aren't mended, if our lives aren't in order, it's going to be hard for us to satisfactorily dress our families.

Jesus talked about the clothes that really matter. "If you decide for God, living a life of God-worship, it follows that you don't fuss about what's on the table at mealtimes or whether the clothes in your closet are in fashion. There is far more to your life than the food you put in your stomach, more to your outer appearance than the clothes you hang on your body. Look at the birds, free and unfettered, not tied down to a job description, careless in the care of God. And you count far more to him than birds....Instead of looking at the fashions, walk out into the fields and look at the wildflowers. They never primp or shop, but have you ever seen color and design quite like it? The ten best-dressed men and women in the country look shabby alongside them. If God gives such attention to the appearance of wildflowers—most of which are never even seen—don't you think he'll attend to you, take pride in you, do his best for you?" (Matthew 6:25–30 *The Message*).

I learned to sew on my grandmother's treadle sewing machine. Her husband worked for the railroad. One day a train came through with a load of sewing machines, and my grandfather traded a pig for one of the machines. That treasure still sits in my guest room. The first apron mother helped me make was from chicken feed sacks. After Daddy died, I found a housecoat Mother had made for him hanging in his closet. Those memories help me relate to Miriam the seamstress.

The 18th verse assures us that Miriam is in no hurry to go to bed, and her candle doesn't go out at night. Jesus said, "I am the light." What happens at night? It is dark, and scary things go bump in the dark. If a mother's light does not go out at night, she keeps the Light shining all the time. We are His candlesticks, keeping His light bright for those in our care.

A familiar sight on the reservation is a Navajo woman sitting on a sheepskin rug in front of her weaving loom. She shears the sheep, cards, dyes, and spins the wool, and builds her own loom. She has no pattern except the design in her mind. She begins weaving and, one strand at a time, the pattern on the beautiful Navajo rug emerges for others to see.

To me, this is a beautiful picture of God's working in our lives. He has a plan for our lives, but it is only revealed to us one yarn—one experience—at a time. Only as we look back can we begin to see the pattern He was creating all along. I'm so thankful that God allows us to have a part in His wonderful plan for our lives.

CHAPTER EIGHT

Supermoms

SERVE GOLDEN APPLES

Humpty Dumpty sat on a wall.
Humpty Dumpty had a great fall.
All the king's horses, and all the king's men
Couldn't put Humpty together again.

Jacque ran into the house with a butterfly encased in her muddy hands. "Now look what you've done—you got your shoes dirty and we're almost ready to go," Mother scolded.

Paul spilled his milk—for the third time that day. "You must be the clumsiest person in the world."

Renee asked, "How do I put this together?"

"I've told you three times already. Now use your stupid head."

This morning I went to the post office. As I approached the door, a mother was leaving with her son, about five years old, a few steps behind her. With a sparkle in his eye, the little boy gallantly held the door open for me. I curtsied slightly and said, "Why, thank you, sir!" just as his mother called sharply, "Come on, Robbie. Let's go." Robbie's smile faded as he dutifully walked off with his mother.

All the king's horses and all the king's men cannot put Humpty together again. And all the king's horses and all the king's men can't remove the harm done by a few harsh or unthinking words. So many times the writer of Proverbs refers to the power of words to harm or heal, to develop or destroy.

- "Worry is a heavy burden, but a kind word always brings cheer" (Proverbs 12:25 CEV).
- "A kind answer soothes angry feelings, but harsh words stir them up" (Proverbs 15:1 CEV).
- "Kind words are good medicine, but deceitful words can really hurt" (Proverbs 15:4 CEV).
- "Giving the right answer at the right time makes everyone happy" (Proverbs 15:23 CEV).
- "You can persuade others if you are wise and speak sensibly. Kind words are like honey—they cheer you up and make you feel strong" (Proverbs 16:23–24 CEV).
- "Watching what you say can save you a lot of trouble" (Proverbs 21:23 CEV).
- "Patience and gentle talk can convince a ruler and overcome any problem" (Proverbs 25:15 CEV).
- "A word fitly spoken is like apples of gold in settings of silver" (Proverbs 25:11 NKJV).

What are the names of some of those Golden Apples? How about "I love you," "I'm sorry," "I forgive you"? One of those apples every day just might keep the doctor away! There are some rotten apples in the basket, too—some apples we want to throw away before they spoil all the other apples. You've tasted them, those apples named "I told you so," "You always..." and "You never..."

Of course James picked right up on the idea when he wrote, "A word out of your mouth may seem of no account, but it can accomplish nearly anything—or destroy it! It only takes a spark, remember, to set off a forest fire. A careless or wrongly placed word out of your mouth can do that. By our speech we can ruin the world, turn harmony to chaos, throw mud on a reputation, send the whole world up in smoke....This is scary: You can tame a tiger, but you can't tame a tongue—it's never been done. The tongue runs wild, a wanton killer. With our tongues we bless God our Father; with the same tongues we curse the very men and women he made in his image. Curses and blessings out of the same mouth! My friends, this can't go on. A spring doesn't gush fresh water one day and brackish the next, does it? Apple trees don't bear strawberries, do they? Raspberry bushes don't bear apples, do they?" (James 3:5–12 *The Message*).

Our own Miriam "opens her mouth with skillful and godly Wisdom, and on her tongue is the law of kindness [giving counsel and instruction]" (Proverbs 31:26 AMP). Or as Peterson says plainly, "When she speaks she has something worthwhile to say, and she always says it kindly" (*The Message*).

You get the idea. The words we speak are immeasurably powerful. When I read these verses, I pause to think about words I have spoken recently. I heard someone say that he always had shoe-leather breath because he puts his foot in his mouth so often. Maybe true supermoms always "engage brain before engaging mouth," but many of the rest of us have trouble in this area.

Have you ever visited Ripley's Believe It or Not museum in Orlando, Florida? Soon after you go into the building, there are pictures of unusual shapes people can make with their tongues. Beside the pictures stands a mirror where you can try making these shapes with your tongue. You twist, turn, and make all kinds of funny faces trying to imitate the pictures. Then you leave that area and tour several more rooms.

Suddenly you come around a corner and discover something you really wish you hadn't seen! The "mirror" near the entrance is actually a one-way window. You now are watching others as they go through the same tongue-twisting antics that you did! Then, in horror, you realize that while you were making those contortions, someone was watching you!

The words that come out of our mouths can come back to us later, just like this one-way window. When we are talking, we don't fully realize how our words will sound when they are received. At the museum I found myself wanting to go back to the entrance and this time act in a more dignified manner! In life, I sometimes find myself wanting to go back to a conversation or situation and respond in a gentler, kinder, more loving way.

THE WRONG WORDS

Part of the problem is that we can't just hit the delete button after we've said something we wish we could take back. Do you read the cartoon strip *Hagar the Horrible*? In the first frame of one issue, Hagar made some derogatory remark about his wife Helga's dress. In the second frame she promptly beat him senseless. And in the last frame he looks at the reader and says, "I knew it was wrong the minute I said it." I've been there, haven't you? Probably didn't get beat up, but sure wanted to hit myself!

Our pastor while we were in seminary was a master at beginning his messages with attention-getting introductions. I shall never forget the Sunday when he stepped into the pulpit and his first sentence was, "Has anyone ever poured cold water on your enthusiasm?"

He proceeded to tell about this *wonderful* message he had spent weeks preparing. He studied at the seminary library, visited with professors about the idea, wrote and re-wrote, and finally gave the manuscript to his secretary to be typed. Then, on Saturday evening, he said, he took his message to the final authority—his wife. She listened patiently, then said, "But honey, you can't preach that tomorrow. That's the Sunday school lesson!"

"She certainly poured cold water on my enthusiasm," he said. Then he proceeded to preach a sermon on that very subject; I've never forgotten it. How often do we drown someone's enthusiasm by the words we say, or even by unspoken communication?

Most children enjoy drawing. When they are very young we ohh and ahh over the multi-colored squiggly lines. (Unless those squiggly lines are on the dining room wall or inside the library book you are reading.) Then they start to school and receive a coloring book as a birthday present. Suddenly squiggly marks are supposed to fit inside predefined lines. We may not say that in so many words; instead we use the positive approach. "Look how well you stayed inside the lines!"

Or the budding artist takes a blank sheet of paper and draws a gray flower with purple leaves on orange grass. "Your flower should be pink or red, not gray, and everyone knows leaves and grass are green." Just a bit of constructive criticism will surely help the child become a better artist and see the world in proper perspective, right? Wrong.

Undoing the damage after you've spoken those harsh words is a hard thing to do. Even though we laugh about it, my heart hurts a bit when I remember a time when I said some words that could not be deleted. One of fourth-grade Nita's favorite afterschool snacks was cottage cheese. One afternoon as she was going out the door to play with Dana she called back, "Mama, I put Dr. Pepper on all the cottage cheese."

"Why in the world did you do that?" I demanded. "Now you've ruined it for everyone else."

"No, I haven't," she protested. "You do that all the time."

"I've *never* done that, and I can't believe you did," I responded.

A couple of hours later, as I was fixing supper, I opened the cottage cheese container, expecting to see white lumps swimming in Dr. Pepper. There was no Dr. Pepper—just a little *salt* and pepper. I begged her forgiveness, and though she said it was okay, it was hard for me to forgive me!

Many years later I was on a trans-Atlantic flight on South Africa Airlines. The flight attendant, a handsome young South African man with a heavy British accent, asked what I would like to drink. Thinking it would probably be my last chance to have one for a while, I asked, "Do you have any Dr. Pepper?"

"Salt and pepper?" he asked, amazed.

"It's okay—I'll just have a Coke." Of course I made certain that Nita heard that story when I got back home from that trip!

When you blow it (and you will if you haven't already), ask God's forgiveness, then ask your children to forgive you. That's a hard thing to do, but there is such healing in those three little words, "I am sorry." Children of all ages (and other people too!) need to hear those words. Healing has begun in many wounded families after one person becomes vulnerable enough to ask for forgiveness. Then, when you've been forgiven, move on to forgive yourself.

THE RIGHT WORDS

So often we aren't aware of the power of our words. Even when they are the right words—the golden apples—we just "serve" them unawares. Have you ever had someone (your own children included) tell you how much something you said long ago meant to them, or how much it helped them make a decision? I always get goose bumps when that happens. And

I am thankful that I just happened to say the right words that time.

Grandson Jeremy was six years old when he had the chicken pox. Now that in itself isn't so dramatic, but here's where I come into the picture. Mother Rhonda was in the hospital, so Jeremy was at my house when he got sick. He was covered with sores from head to toe and everywhere in between. He and I spent one l-o-n-g night on the trundle bed—him on the lower pullout bed and me on the top bed, rubbing his little sore-covered body with powder and calamine lotion. It was 5:00 A.M. when we both finally went to sleep.

Several months later, something caused him to think of that experience, and he asked, "Nana, do you remember how much fun we had that night when I had chicken pox?" I was so thankful God had given me patience, a grandson, and a bottle of calamine lotion.

There are so many good words we need to speak. Words of encouragement. "Good job." "You go, girl." Words of affirmation. Words of gentle instruction. And there are so many words we must leave unspoken—nagging, criticizing, gossiping, bitter, and complaining words.

There are some very powerful words that we need to use frequently. One of those is *thank you.* I kept little Jeremy during the day while Rhonda was taking some college classes. I guess I don't fit the grandmother stereotype: I don't always do everything my grandchildren want me to do! Reba tells me that I need not have any illusions of ever winning the Grandmother of the Year award.

Anyway, Jeremy decided mid-morning that he wanted some oatmeal. Now that in itself is not such a big request, but the timing was not the greatest. I needed to go to the store; I had just cleaned the kitchen; I had to open a new box of oatmeal (big deal). I did fix his oatmeal, but not too happily, I'm afraid. He ate every bite (he really was hungry!) and we left for the store. On the way he said quietly, "Nana, thank you for making me oatmeal."

With tears in my eyes I reached over and took his little hand in mine. "Thank you for saying thank you," I said. I was reminded that I, too, need to frequently say "thank you" to others who serve me when they may not really want to.

There's another phrase that we need to use when appropriate—*I'm sorry*. I have always enjoyed listening to Paul Harvey's "News and Comments." One part I especially look forward to is his salute to couples who have been married for a long time. Once I heard him tell about a couple who were celebrating their 67th anniversary. In his inimitable way, Harvey said, "Hmm. Just think how many 'I'm sorrys' and 'I forgive yous' it took to live together that long."

For some reason, it is often very difficult for us as parents to tell our children that we are sorry. Admitting we were wrong might make us vulnerable and diminish our place of authority, we fear. So many parents try to say "I'm sorry" without using those words. They joke about the situation, or try to make up for the incident in other ways. Yet nothing is as healing and strong as the spoken words.

Do you remember how "cool" The Fonz was on the television show *Happy Days*? Once, when he was caught in a mistake, he tried to confess. Instead, it came out, "I was wroooo." "I was wrrrooo." He tried several times but never did manage to get out the words *I was wrong*. It is hard to say those three words, but they can be the medicine that heals a wounded heart (Proverbs 15:4).

The word processing program I use has a wonderful feature. When I enter an incorrectly spelled word, the computer (thinks it's smarter than I am!) places a red line beneath that word. I depend so much on that feature that I often don't check to see if perhaps I've entered an incorrect word, but one that is spelled correctly, for example *their* instead of *there.* Recently, I was handwriting a note. I was not sure that I had spelled a word correctly, so I automatically looked to see if there was a red line beneath it. No line—must be spelled correctly! But not necessarily.

I have sometimes wished that we could rehearse some of the things we say, and if the words were inappropriate, harsh, damaging, or unnecessary, a red line would appear, or a quiet alarm would sound. We could return to the word or phrase, change or delete it completely, then hit the send button. That's impossible, of course, so we must be very careful when we open our mouths to speak.

FAMILY TRIVIA

One of my writing ventures was a Family Tree-via game. Players were asked to answer questions such as "Tell about a time when you got in trouble at school." "What was your favorite food when you were a child?" "What was your maternal grandmother's maiden name?" We used the game at a family reunion and I even sold a few!

I sent one of the games to Perry and Kelley while they were working as student missionaries in New York City. One evening they invited another young couple to their apartment and they played "Family Tree-via." The next morning the guest went to the hospital to visit his father who had just had some minor surgery. The young man decided to ask his dad some of those same questions, and he learned things about his father, his heritage, and his own life that he never knew. Just a few days later, the father passed away. Grateful that he had that visit with his father, the young man told Kelley, "I never would have known those things if it hadn't been for that game."

We must take time to talk to our children, no matter what their ages. I will always cherish the last night that I spent in my daddy's house with him. A couple of days later he went to the hospital for the final two weeks of his life. That special night we stayed up until almost midnight. He was telling me about his homesteading adventures in New Mexico. I'd heard many of the stories before, but less than a month later, when I looked at his voiceless body, I was so glad that I had heard the stories one more time.

Just a few days before my mother died I stood beside her hospital bed, both of us knowing that her life was almost over. What do you say to someone so dear to you when you know you'll never see her again in this life? She said, "Talk to me. Tell me about yourself." She knew everything about me! But she wanted to hear one more time about her grandchildren, about the work I loved, about the life I had chosen.

Happy words are good, too. Tell funny things that happened to you. Don't be a grouch. Our family laughs a lot—so much, in fact, that when the girls and I get together the sons-in-law just roll their eyes and retreat to another room! Of course, be sure your humor is appropriate. Don't make fun of your children or ridicule them for things they say or do, but help them be able to laugh at themselves. Sometimes a touch of humor is the oil that can calm some troubled waters.

Mothers not only need wise tongues; they need listening hearts. Verse 26 is about speaking; verse 27 could be about remaining silent: "She keeps an eye on everyone in her household, and keeps them all busy and productive" (*The Message*). How can she know what is going on with her family if she isn't listening—really listening? One of my coworkers has a bumper sticker that reads, "My wife says I don't listen to her—or something like that." Our children can "rattle" a lot, and it is easy to turn them off in our minds while pretending to be listening.

Brenda and Kay were visiting while their children played in the other room. Cody had already interrupted her several times with trivial questions, so when he asked one more question, she absentmindedly replied, "Sure. Go ahead."

Just a few minutes later they heard a scream coming from the living room.

"What happened?"

"I bit him," Cody replied.

"WHY?" Brenda demanded.

"You *told* me I could."

Words aren't the only way we communicate, of course. Often actions speak louder than words. Have your teenagers ever rolled their eyes at you? Didn't that speak volumes? Sometimes just a hug or a friendly touch can communicate a lot to our children. We all have those special family facial expressions that communicate hidden messages, too. My three and I had a signal when they were with friends. If the friend asked, "Can she come home with me?" my child would give me the "yes-I-want-to" or the "no-I-don't-want-to" look. I had a special wink/nose wrinkle that meant "It's okay; don't worry." Then of course there is that "Don't even think about it" look that gets a lot of use.

Perry and Kelley were so excited about the coming of their daughter Laney. Jordan was two, and the pregnancy had been normal so far as anyone knew. I was on the phone when the operator interrupted my call with an emergency call. It was Perry. "Mama, we have problems. Laney isn't okay."

After three weeks of tubes, wires, masks, and needles, Laney's little body rested in Jesus' arms. What does a mother say to her son when he is standing in the ICU looking at his dying daughter? Nothing. She just holds him tight and wishes, oh how she wishes more than anything in the world, that she could make the hurt go away.

TIME FOR TALKING

Time spent working together can be a great time for talking. Although I've loved having a dishwasher (you met Lucy earlier), I remember some good talks I had with my children as we washed dishes together. Traveling is also a good time for talking—especially once you get past the "Don't make me have to stop and take off my belt" and "How much farther?" conversations.

Talk to your children about spiritual things. Read the Bible with them. Talk about what they learned in Sunday school. Help them form opinions and ideas about who they are and Whose they are. Pray with them. Pray for them. Pray about them.

We are supposed to have all the answers, and just the right words. The truth is, there are times when there are no words that are right. One of Nita's dogs died happy—he loved to chase cars, and he finally caught one. Her heart was broken. Darren doesn't make the team. Carrie's first love ends in tears. A marriage ends in a bitter divorce. That too-good-to-be-true job offer was too good to be true.

Use the words "I love you" liberally. One of my teenagers had done something to displease me. After we had our mother/child encounter, I hugged her and said, "I love you."

"Even though I make mistakes?" she asked. I assured her that I did.

Our children need to know they can trust us not to betray confidences, or to talk about them to other people. If they learn this as young children, they are more apt to trust us with confidences as they grow older. On the other hand, be careful about boasting to others about how perfect your children are. No one will believe you anyway!

I went to the hospital with a 69-year-old woman while she had a heart catheterization. I knew that she had a difficult life, but my own heart ached with what she told me. As they were putting her into the ambulance to take her to the hospital, her 88-year-old mother leaned down, kissed her, and said, "I love you."

My friend said, "That was the first time Mama ever told me she loved me. Why did she have to wait so long?"

Children are listening! They are going to repeat what you say, or at least what they think you said. One Sunday Perry and Kelley were in the kitchen fixing lunch. They heard Joel singing in the living room, "He is exhausted, the King is exhausted." (The song said that God is *exalted*.)

I was giving perms to my daughters. Two-year-old Kendyl was sitting at the table with us. Looking in the mirror, she ran the comb through her hair, looked admiringly at her reflection, and asked, "Do I look younger?"

Mother used to tell the story about the woman who always had something good to say about everyone. One day Mr. Jones died. The neighbor women said, "She surely can't say anything good about *him*. He was a cheat, a thief, and the grouchiest man in town." They hurried over to her house with the news and waited for her response.

"What a shame. And he could whistle so pretty."

Yes, supermoms serve golden apples—always speaking words that are just right. I confess again—as long as I can talk I'll say things I shouldn't say and wish I hadn't said. I'll speak when I should be listening. I'll have a hard time saying "Forgive me. I'm sorry. I was wrong." But my prayer, like the psalmist, is that "the words of my mouth and the meditation of my heart be pleasing in your sight, O Lord, my Rock and my Redeemer" (Psalm 19:14).

CHAPTER NINE

Supermoms
CLIMB MOUNTAINS

"It was a dark and stormy night...." It really was. Winters in western New Mexico can be really wicked. The low temperature that night was 15 degrees below zero. I remember that fact, like so many other trivial facts from that night.

Rhonda had graduated from high school that spring and was living at home, working at a convenience store less than half a mile from our house. Against my advice and wishes, the manager sometimes left her alone to close at night. This was one of those nights.

She closed out the cash register, turned out the inside lights, locked the door behind her, and went around the corner of the building to turn off the main switch. Suddenly, a man jumped out of the darkness. He was holding a butcher knife in one hand; he grabbed her with the other hand. Forcing her into her waiting car, he held the knife to her throat as he made her drive out onto the snow-covered prairie, where he raped her.

I woke up just about the time she was to close, but knew that she planned to drive into town to visit some friends. I wasn't especially worried about her, but did feel a strong need to pray for her. My prayer was that God would protect her, thinking the wintry weather was her greatest enemy. Then I fell back to sleep.

Shortly after midnight I was awakened by the sounds of her muffled cries. That night grew even darker and colder as she told us what had happened. The remainder of the night was spent making police reports and a hospital visit, and cruising through town in the police car in search of the rapist.

I know little about mountain climbing, but I know enough to know that a good rope is an essential piece of equipment. In chapter four I told you about the peace that I experienced just a few days after that terrible night. Had I not had a Father to lean on, to be the rope that I could hang on to, I'm not sure how I would have survived the days—and weeks—that followed.

How would a supermom climb a mountain like this? I'm not sure, but I think she might have known just what to do, just what to say to her daughter and others, just how to handle her own turbulent emotions. As I've confessed—I am no supermom. I basically fell apart.

The mountain looming before me was more forbidding than Mt. Everest. I did not want to climb it; I didn't even want to look at it. I wanted to turn around and run the other direction as fast as I could. Yet there was no choice. The mountain was there; there was no way around, through, or under it. I had to begin climbing.

Climbing mountains is certainly not my idea of fun. It's right up there with swimming the English Channel, running the Boston Marathon, or saddle-breaking a bucking horse. I would imagine if the truth were known, all mothers at some time or another have had to climb mountains they didn't want to climb. We all, at some time, face a problem that we don't want to face; have to endure an experience that hurts to the very core of our existence.

Perry was five when we went to watch his cousin John run in a track meet. John had won several events, but when he ran the high hurdles he came in a close second. Perry watched in fascination as they ran, but when the race was over and John had not won, Perry said indignantly, "Well, if they'd just gotten those things out of his way, John could have won." Haven't you wished you could get some of life's high hurdles out of your way so you wouldn't have to jump them?

Lana was mother to three healthy little boys when Calvin was born. His birth defects meant that he would never walk, talk, or develop mentally beyond infancy. For 15 years Lana has lifted, bathed, fed, and loved this special child. She had to climb that mountain. No choice.

Her experience reminded me of the illustration I once heard from a woman whose story was similar. She said it was as though she woke up to find herself on a flight to Los Angeles, but her ticket was for Chicago. She didn't want to go to Los Angeles, but she had no choice. That's where the plane was headed.

Al came home from work one day and told Martha he wanted a divorce. Martha knew there had been some problems, but she had no idea he had been having an affair with a coworker in his office. She and her two children found themselves facing a mountain that had to be climbed.

Ellen's daughter Kari ran away from home when she was 18, and Ellen has not seen her for over 20 years. She has heard through friends that Kari is gay and that she has multiple sclerosis. But Kari doesn't want to come home, and she has made it understood that she does not want to see Ellen again.

Not all our mountains are this ominous, of course. Some mountains are really hills that come in the form of stopped up toilets, broken legs, and snow days when the kids can't go to school and can't go outside to play. One week when Dalton was gone to a conference, my washing machine stopped washing, my car wouldn't start, and all three kids had tonsillitis. Rhonda considered all our circumstances and asked, "Mama, is it true that when Daddy leaves home, God goes with him?"

The Gaithers have a song called "The Christ of Every Crisis." I believe He is, and that we can pray about everything. What better resource is there for mothers than prayer? When some of our friends were buying a house I made some comment about their praying about the decision. They told me that they didn't think we should bother God about things like that. I disagree.

I guess my prayer life is more like that of my friend Margaret. We were sitting together at a conference. The conference leader gave us a writing assignment. When I asked what she was writing, Margaret replied that she was writing a letter to God. She explained that she prayed so much about so many things she imagined He got tired of listening to her all the time. She said that He probably thought, "Oh, no, it's *her* again!" So she frequently wrote Him prayer letters that He could read when He had time!

BACKGROUND MUSIC

I have an idea that I think would help us ordinary mothers when we encounter mountains—both the menacing ones and the oversized speed bumps—that we have to climb. We need background music for our real-life sitcoms and soap operas. Soft strings would accompany romantic moments; a banjo or honky-tonk piano would play "The Entertainer" during life's fun times. When something frightening is about to happen the music would crescendo mysteriously, and when the danger is past, the music would decrescendo back to a soft melody. If it were going to be a really scary scene, the music would be the theme from the movie "Jaws."

Mothers could use pre-drama music to a definite advantage. The abrasive sound of a ringing phone awakens you in the middle of the night, and you have no idea what you're about to face. A little background music to wake us up and give some idea of the impending crisis would help!

Another good thing about background music would be the time-outs for advertising. Just think how many conversations we could rehearse if the music signaled that "now it's time for a word from our sponsor." Like Scarlett in *Gone with the Wind*, we could think about that tomorrow. Then when it was time to resume the drama at hand, a theme song would alert us to the fact that we'd better take our places and get ready to pick up where we left off.

I think perhaps supermoms do have background music. That's why they know when to move and when to stop, when to run and when to walk. That's why they say the right words at the right time—they plan those speeches during station identification breaks.

While my life (like yours) certainly does not have background music effects, music has certainly helped me climb a lot of mountains. So often a familiar hymn sung at church or on the radio is just what I need to hear. Sometimes, if the mountain isn't too tall, I can hum or sing a hymn and find that I am already feeling better. (I like to "Whistle While I Work," but only when no one else is around to hear me!)

A few summers ago I had the privilege of attending the National Southern Baptist Deaf Convention. One evening the husband of the woman who was to bring the special music led her to the platform. Taking her hand, he signed into her palm that she could begin. You see, she was both deaf and blind. There in that quiet auditorium she began to sign, then an unseen interpreter began singing these words: "Jesus is all the world to me, my life, my joy, my all; He is my strength from day to day, without Him I would fall." My life has never been quite the same since that night. When I have a mountain that I think I just can't face, I often sing that song and think of her.

David had some pretty big mountains to climb, too. He had been running from his enemies when he wrote Psalm 5. "Listen GOD! Please, pay attention! Can you make sense of these ramblings, my groans and cries? King-God, I need your help. Every morning you'll hear me at it again. Every morning I lay out the pieces of my life on your altar and watch for fire to descend. And here I am, your invited guest—it's incredible! I enter your house; here I am, prostrate in your inner sanctum, waiting for directions to get me safely through enemy lines" (Psalm 5:1–3, 7–8 *The Message*).

We have laughed in this chapter about those monstrous mountains we have to climb, but sometimes laughter is the only way we can get over them. Sometimes they are just too forbidding for us to face otherwise. The Proverbs 31 mother's "lamp goes not out, but it burns on continually through the night [of trouble, privation, or sorrow, warning away fear, doubt, and distrust]" (Proverbs 31:18b AMP).

Sometimes we have to just keep hanging on, just keep the light burning, knowing that morning will come. The psalmist claimed God's promise that "Weeping may endure for a night, but joy comes in the morning" (Psalm 30:5b AMP). Eugene Peterson says it this way: "The nights of crying your eyes out give way to days of laughter" (*The Message*).

Even Paul picked up this theme: "So we're not giving up. How could we! Even though on the outside it often looks like things are falling apart on us, on the inside, where God is making new life, not a day goes by without his unfolding grace. These hard times are small potatoes compared to the coming good times, the lavish celebration prepared for us. There's far more here than meets the eye. The things we see now are here today, gone tomorrow. But the things we can't see now will last forever" (2 Corinthians 4:16–18 *The Message*).

Christ will give us the strength to face anything that comes our way, to climb any mountain that lies before us. "God reminds us, I heard your call in the nick of time; the day you needed me, I was there to help" (2 Corinthians 6:2 *The Message*).

How do you climb a mountain? One step at a time. Take a step of faith toward that mountain, then another, then another. Supermoms may try climbing mountains by themselves, and they may even make it halfway to the top. But the mother facing 21st century-sized mountains has a resource far greater than those who try to do it on their own. We have the God of the universe as our climbing partner.

In his closing prayer last Sunday, my pastor prayed, "Thank you for all we're experiencing right now." I thought of women in our congregation—Karen's husband recovering from a serious stroke, Myra's husband with Alzheimer's, Margie with her son in jail, Doris raising her grandchildren while her daughter is in drug rehab, Jennie who just found out she has cancer, Carol who has fought Parkinson's Disease for 18 years. Those are some pretty awesome mountains.

Yet we serve a God who is able to carry us through these difficult times. I love the response of Shadrach, Meshach, and Abednego when King Nebuchadnezzar threatened to throw them into the furnace: "Your threat means nothing to us. If you throw us in the fire, the God we serve can rescue us from your roaring furnace and anything else you might cook up, O king. But even if he doesn't, it wouldn't make a bit of difference, O king" (Daniel 3:17–18 *The Message*). One preacher interprets this story like this: "Our God is able to rescue us. And even if He doesn't, He's still able."

Just think of the joy we miss if we walk with our Savior only in the sunlight. A few years ago a popular song said that

"If I'd never had a problem, I wouldn't know that He could solve them." Some of the sweetest fellowship we have with Him is when He walks with us through the valleys—when He holds our hand so we can make it through the darkest night.

The prophet Habakkuk knew about difficult times, but after much complaining, he finally ended his conversation with God in a prayer of praise. "Though the cherry trees don't blossom and the strawberries don't ripen, though the apples are worm-eaten and the wheat fields stunted, though the sheep pens are sheepless and the cattle barns empty, I'm singing joyful praise to GOD. I'm turning cartwheels of joy to my Savior God. Counting on GOD's Rule to prevail, I take heart and gain strength. I run like a deer. I feel like I'm king of the mountain!" (Habakkuk 3:17–19 *The Message*).

- "Always use the name of our Lord Jesus Christ to thank God the Father for everything" (Ephesians 5:20 CEV).
- "Always be joyful and never stop praying. Whatever happens, keep thanking God because of Jesus Christ. This is what God wants you to do" (1 Thessalonians 5:16–18 CEV).

And of course, we so often claim the promise that "God is always at work for the good of everyone who loves him. They are the ones God has chosen for His purpose" (Romans 8:28 CEV).

Thank Him for the mountains? In *all* things give thanks? Only when we keep that light burning continually through the night of trouble, chasing away sorrow, sadness, fear, doubt, and distrust can we do that. Go climb that mountain, my friend.

CHAPTER TEN

Supermoms
ARE RABBITS

All mothers are *not* created equal. They come in different sizes and shapes, with different abilities, different personalities, and different interests. But all mothers do have one thing in common—they each have 24 hours in a day. However, I think some mothers must have 25 hours in their days. How else can they do all they do? Prepare at least two nutritious meals (cleaning the kitchen after each one), polish the silver (does anyone really do that anymore?), wash the windows, run the vacuum, wash, dry, fold, hang, iron, and put up five loads of laundry, work eight hours at her "other" job, have the SUV serviced, and work out at the gym.

Non-supermoms, on the other hand, have reality days. One of my friends says that she knows she's had a productive day when realizes she managed to get both her legs shaved on the same day. Linda says she leaves her vacuum cleaner sitting in the middle of the living room. When someone comes to see her, she explains, "I was just about to vacuum." Some women collect teddy bears or salt and pepper shakers—others of us collect dust. My mother used to say it was okay to write your name in the dust—just don't date it. Carol's home was burglarized. After the police came she filled out an insurance claim form listing everything that was taken—microwave, TV, jewelry, stereo. Three months later she discovered that her vacuum cleaner was also gone. I've already told you where Dalton hides my Christmas gifts—in the oven. He knows I'll never look there. I think you have the picture—not one of these women (me included) qualifies as a supermom.

It's hard not to think of the Proverbs 31 mother as a supermom. Just look at all she accomplished in her 24-hour day. "First thing in the morning, she dresses for work, rolls up her sleeves, eager to get started. She senses the worth of her work, is in no hurry to call it quits for the day" (Proverbs 31:17-18 *The Message*). She shops for the best buys, cooks meals, plans the day's work for her servant girls, buys a field, then plants a garden on it, helps someone who has a need, sews garments for herself and her family, and makes a few extras to sell. And that's just what she does on Monday!

When I have a gotta-get-it-done-now day, Dalton sometimes tells me, "You don't have to conquer the world all in one day." I have an idea that Miriam didn't do all of the above in just one day, either. Perhaps a week, or a month, or even a year. But I believe she must have balanced her daily tasks with those other short-range and long-range projects in order to do it all.

I'm sure you remember the story of the tortoise and the hare. While the rabbit was dashing about enjoying the advantages of his speed, the turtle was calmly, progressively moving toward the goal. Somehow I picture the hare as the supermom and the tortoise as the ordinary, everyday mother who steadily and with purpose does the work at hand.

The rabbit, dashing madly toward the finish line, will miss the fragrant flowers blooming along the path. She won't hear the bird's whistle or the gurgling stream. She won't hear God's invitation to "Be still, and know that I am God" (Psalm 46:10 NKJV) or, as the CEV says, "Calm down, and learn that I am God!" *The Message* tells us to "Step out of the traffic! Take a long, loving look at me, your High God." I see turtle tracks all over these verses, don't you?

I believe, in the long run, Turtle Moms are going to win the race. But how? Becky has a plaque in her kitchen that reads, "I'm too busy to be organized." While I can appreciate the humor, every time I see it I think, I'm too busy *not* to be organized. For several years I have led time management conferences, which I call Time Investment Seminars. My theory is that time is like money: it can be spent, wasted, or invested. I like to get the maximum return on my money, and I also like to get the maximum return on my time. If I wisely invest my time, I don't have be a supermom in order to get the most out of the 24-hour days I have been given.

Good time management is also good stewardship. Our time is a gift from God, and it belongs to Him. We should guard it carefully, enjoy it fully, use it wisely, and give thanks for it continually. In Ephesians 5:16 we are told to redeem the time. In *Trusted Steward,* Calvin Partain writes, "Redeem means 'paying a price to recover from the power of another.' Wise use of time is not automatic. We must pay a price, expend effort, set priorities, and make plans to redeem time. Otherwise we become the victim of the clock and the calendar, and the evil times in which we live will set our agenda. To let time slip by unredeemed is to let life slip by unredeemed."

STRESS MANAGERS

Good time managers are also usually good stress managers. Just practicing a few simple organizational skills can alleviate some of the tensions of an otherwise crazy day. For example, something as trivial as misplacing your car keys can be a major source of stress if you're in a hurry. But by using a clip key-chain you can always find your keys hanging from the strap of your purse.

Speaking of stress—Betty, my nurse friend, gave me three simple steps to take when facing stressful circumstances. They have helped me many times put some situations in perspective. Step 1: Remove the source of stress. If you can, do so. If not, accept that fact and move to Step 2: Remove yourself from the source of stress. Again, do so if you can, and if you can't then move to Step 3: Change your attitude about the situation.

I put this to a test soon after the first time I heard it, and have used it so many times since. We lived just off a busy four-lane highway. In order for me to enter traffic, I had to pull into the right-hand lane. However, oncoming cars would rarely pull into the left lane so I could have my lane, which usually meant a long wait until there was a break in traffic.

Step 1: There was no way I could remove the source. The highway was the only way I had to leave our subdivision, and I certainly couldn't change the driving patterns of others. **Step 2:** I could not remove myself, because that was where our home was. I had to use that road. **Step 3:** Instead of impatiently racing my motor and being frustrated with the other drivers (inconsiderate though they were!), I began counting my blessings as I sat there. Sometimes I would pray for those in the approaching cars; other times I would sing along with a tape. Once I actually realized too late that I had had a chance to pull onto the road and had missed it!

From one turtle to another, I'm going to share with you some things I have found that help me be organized. If you are a supermom, go ahead and race forward, but you'd better not stop to smell the roses, or gloat over your superior skills, or we turtles will pass you and win the race!

SET GOALS

It's been said that if you don't know where you're going, how will you know when you get there? Goals should be both long-range and short-range. Long-range goals are those things you plan to do in six months, a year, five years. Long-range goals are such things as finish a college degree, add a family room to the house, or participate in an overseas mission project.

These may be goals that you will work on a little at a time. After you've set the goal, list those steps that will help you reach the goal. If it is completing that college degree, you will do that one course at a time. It may be that you open a savings or money market account where you can set aside money monthly to help you achieve your goal.

Other goals are short-range. What needs to be accomplished this month? This week? Today? I'm a consummate list-maker—I've even been known to list something that I've already done, just so I can mark it off. Making lists has several advantages. For one thing, a list can reboot your memory chip, reminding you to do something that you might otherwise forget. Lists also help us focus on the important tasks without getting sidetracked by less important ones.

Goals should be SMART—Specific, Measurable, Attainable, Realistic, and Time-oriented. For example, "I want to lose some weight" is neither specific, measurable, nor time oriented. "I want to lose 15 pounds by next Friday" is neither attainable nor realistic. However, a goal to "lose 10 pounds in the next 6 months" meets all five criteria.

You cannot set a goal for someone else any more than someone else can set one for you. We often want to set goals for other family members, but unless they have ownership of the goal, they will never buy into it. By the same token, your husband may want you to lose weight, but I can guarantee you won't lose a pound until that becomes your personal goal.

An authentic supermom's goals might be specific, measurable, and time-oriented, but I seriously doubt they are realistic or attainable. Therein lies a quantifiable difference between supermoms and turtle moms. Reality women know, accept, and deal with their limitations. The woman who is vying for the Supermom of the Year award is determined that she is going to be and do more than she is capable of.

I believe that goal setting might have been Miriam's secret to success. I seriously doubt that every day she sewed, bought property, traded with merchants, and worked in her garden. She may have done different tasks on different days of the week, or done the most important things for that day, but she didn't do everything every day. Which brings us to the next organizational tip.

SET PRIORITIES

I use the A-B-C method to prioritize my daily to-do lists. An A job is something that must be done today. Those are the things to be done first, even if I dread doing them. I might occasionally add a B job that I really want to do, just to give myself a break. Sometimes a B or even a C will suddenly become an A. But having that A list keeps me on track to get done the really necessary things.

There are also times when I find that an A can become a C. Some days you think you *must* vacuum, then your son calls from school and asks if you can watch him run in the track meet. Track meets should win out over vacuuming every time.

My pastor told about spending his childhood summers with his grandparents, who lived on a farm. Every morning they fed the chickens, gathered eggs, slopped the pigs, milked the cows, and took them out to pasture. Then after eating a hearty breakfast Granddad said, "Now it's time to go to work."

"But we've already been working," Richard protested.

"No, son," the wise grandfather replied. "Them was chores. Now we do the work."

Chores—those mundane, tedious, sometimes not-so-fun things that we have to do whether we want to or not. A lot of our days are made up of chores, aren't they? Getting our chores done is a lot like dealing with other stresses in life. Remember? If we can't change the chores, and can't remove ourselves from having to do them, we can at least change our attitude. Instead of complaining because you have to wash dishes, be thankful that your family has enough food to eat. Instead of complaining because you have to go to work, be thankful you have a job. Instead of wishing you didn't have to clean the bathroom, be thankful you have indoor plumbing. I think you get the idea.

Priorities help in setting long-range goals as well. I will put more time, energy, and even financial resources into accomplishing an A priority long-range goal than a C goal. Remember, you're the one who makes the decision about the priority. What to others may seem like a C priority may to you be an A, or vice versa.

DELEGATE

Even if you can't set goals for others, you can ask others to help you accomplish your goals. Back in my try-to-be super-mom days, I thought I was supposed to do all the housecleaning, cooking, laundry, and so forth. I well remember a day when, while all our children were still at home, I was getting ready to leave for a writers conference. I had cooked meals ahead and frozen them, done all the laundry, and was making sure the house was clean. I can still remember this scene: I was on my knees cleaning the bathtub when Rhonda came in. Watching me and knowing I was about to leave, she said, "Mama, you're either awfully sweet or awfully stupid."

Supermom woke up and smelled the coffee, or the bathtub cleaner as the case may have been. I never heard her say she was sorry she had made that comment, but things did begin to change around our house! Now, years later, our nest is empty and I am working full time outside the home. Dalton, who took early retirement so he could go with me for my job, is now my domestic engineer. It's always fun to hear the kids' reaction when they call home and find Daddy washing dishes or folding laundry.

When Shirley went back to the university to work on her doctorate, she and Don made an agreement. Whoever *it* bothered the most would do something about *it*. "It," of course, could have been anything—spider webs on the ceiling, a dirty kitchen floor, the ring around the bathtub. After about three months Don said, "I don't think I like this arrangement. Nothing bothers you anymore!"

We already talked about the maids that today's women enjoy. Delegate as much work to them as possible. Nora and her husband have a nice dishwasher, but they never use it. "We just don't have enough dirty dishes," she says. Dalton and I usually run our dishwasher every other day at least, and sometimes more often than that. I don't mind if Nora doesn't use hers, but I'm certainly going to delegate the responsibility of washing dishes to my Lucy.

Remember what our children are supposed to say when someone asks them if they want to use drugs? "Just say no." That's pretty good advice for us, too. Think of the time you spend wishing you didn't have to do something that you agreed to do. Why did you say yes? Were you trying to please someone else, or feel needed? A commitment to your family or yourself is as much a priority as any other appointment. If asked to help with an event when you don't really want to be involved, it's okay to say, "I already have a commitment."

LOOSE CHANGE TIME

How do you feel about "loose change time"? You know, those five or ten minutes between projects, meetings, or other involvements. Keep blank cards in your purse so you can write a thank you or a note of encouragement to someone while waiting at the doctor's office. Or you might keep your to-do list handy so you can review what you need to work on when you get home. You intended to clean the bathroom during the day but didn't get it done, and now you want to watch a movie on TV. During the commercial give the bathroom a quick scrub. You have just a few minutes before the kids come home from school? Check your email, put a load of clothes in to wash, or dust the coffee table. You are not only making wise use of your loose change time, but this will keep you from spending too much time on a project that shouldn't take but a few minutes.

You may spend your loose change time on yourself, too. Take a five-minute vacation. Pick up a magazine and look through a couple more pages. Do you have a pick-up hobby such as needlework that you can do for just a few minutes? Or perhaps you would rather play the piano or prune your houseplants.

Interruptions are another frustration when you're trying to use your time wisely. The phone rings and it's a telemarketer. But you've had to stop what you were doing and deal with the interruption. That's when answering machines are nice to have! But what about those interruptions you do have to deal with? Sometimes it's okay to say, "I just don't have time right now." Other times we need to realize that this interruption just may have been God's way of slowing us down, or bringing someone into our lives when they need us.

I was really absorbed in writing a Bible study one day when the doorbell rang. We lived right beside a main highway (the one with four lanes!) and on the edge of the reservation.

Each day a number of Native Americans walked along this road going into town, but they didn't usually stop. On this day, however, a man passing by was hungry and stopped by the house to see if I could give him something to eat. My first thought was, "I'm busy! I don't have time to stop and fix him a sandwich." I stopped short when I remembered one verse in my assigned Scripture: "I was hungry and you gave Me food; I was thirsty and you gave Me drink; I was a stranger and you took Me in" (Matthew 25:35 NKJV). I stopped and gave him something to eat, and I'm glad I did.

GETTING ORGANIZED

I've found that getting organized is something that most people either hate or enjoy. I'm one of the latter. I've heard that a clean desk is the sign of a sick mind—well, guess what? I rarely leave work with anything on my desk except my in/out box, a couple of kaleidoscopes, and a Bible beneath a special paperweight. When I do have stacks on my desk, one of my co-workers always stops by to thank me for making him feel better!

There are so many organizational tools we can use. Here are some ideas for you:

▪ **Use a filing cabinet and file folders**. Keep files that you know you might use, but if it's something you're not sure about, toss it. A good rule of thumb is to ask, "What would be the worst thing that could happen if I throw this away?" One woman says that her husband has his pile-its license. "Pile-it here, pile-it there." Give up your pile-its license if you have one!

▪ **Throw things away**. Don't keep a magazine if it has only one article you want to keep. Cut out the article, put it in the appropriate file, and toss the rest of the magazine. Always open your mail beside a trash can, shredding and throwing away all those credit card applications and other junk mail. Put mail that needs your response in one stack (bills and wedding invitations, for example) then set a time when you respond appropriately (by paying the bill or sending a gift).

Take a trash bag and walk through your house collecting things that should be thrown away. Two half-empty lotion bottles? Combine them and throw one away. A cooking fork that you never use because it has a broken handle? Throw it away. The last seven issues of *Reader's Digest*? Penicillin growing in your refrigerator? I think you get the message.

What about those closets? Make three piles—one of things you want to keep, one for things to be given away, and one for trash. When you've finished, you'll enjoy looking at your closet and you'll be able to find what you do decide to keep.

■ **Take time off.** Part of good time management is taking time off, time for ourselves. Do you feel guilty when you take a *real* day off? You know, the kind when you sleep late if you want, take your kids to the park or your grandchildren to the zoo, go to the mall to look for a new blouse. If so, don't! Supermoms may not take days off, but a wise Proverbs 31 mom does. Give yourself a gift of time.

Perhaps you want to take up a new hobby. I love to cross-stitch. When I began this hobby I had a high-stress job; I took work home almost every evening. Cross-stitch enabled me to be totally engrossed in something besides work.

■ **Take time to grow and be renewed.** Bill Hybels wrote a book called *Too Busy Not to Pray*. Spend time with your Father in prayer and Bible study. Read other books, too. Learn something new. Exercise your mind!

■ **Don't procrastinate**. One of the biggest time thieves is procrastination. It's that simple. When I lead Time Investment Seminars and come to this subject, people always snicker or moan. Procrastination is a habit, and not a very good one. Why do people procrastinate? There are several reasons. If we dread something, we think that by not doing it, we can avoid the inevitable. It will have to be done eventually; why not go ahead and get it over with, and then you don't have to dread it?

Another reason for procrastination is perfectionism. Remember my grandmother's advice that "Be the labor great or small, do it well or not at all"? I don't have time to clean the house well, so I just won't do anything. Why not do one thing now and the rest later when you do have time?

Fear of failure can also cause us to procrastinate. Lisa wanted to go back to college, but she was afraid she wouldn't be able to make it, so she kept finding excuses not to take that step. One way to be sure you never fail at anything is never to try. I love these lines from the movie *Chariots of Fire*: "If I can't win, I won't run." The reply: "If you don't run, you can't win."

■ **Balance your life**. Have some time for work, some for pleasure, some for pure fun. I'm not sure what Miriam did for relaxation, but I have a feeling she could laugh, play, and enjoy life as well as all the "industrious" things she did. Too much of most things is too much. Sometimes we have no control over the demands on our time, but even then we need to look for ways to find balance.

■ **Capitalize on your talents and abilities**. In other words, do what you are good at. Mary tole paints beautifully. While they were visiting us I picked up my cross-stitch as we waited on our husbands to take us to dinner. Mary's hobby, on the other hand, requires that she get out all her paints, so it's not a pick-up hobby. Yet she tried cross-stitching and didn't care for it at all, and I have absolutely no painting abilities. If you don't enjoy what you're doing, perhaps you need to do something else.

An 85-year-old woman was attending one of my time investment retreats. After I had talked about this subject—about doing what you enjoyed, she told me she had always wanted to paint, and had just decided she was going to take lessons! Sure enough, she did, and the next time I saw her she gave me one of her paintings. It might not win any blue ribbons, but to me it's priceless. It reminds me that we should capture the joy in each day while we have it.

My mother-in-law made quilts for all her family, and I became fascinated with the art of quilting. While we were living on the Navajo reservation I found that quilting was a great way to spend time with other women, and many of the Navajo women did not know how to quilt. We got word that an older Anglo couple was planning to come spend the day with us. Not sure what we would talk about, I thought, "At least she'll probably be interested in quilting. We can talk about that."

They hadn't been there long when I asked, "Do you quilt?"

She replied bluntly, "No. I never could see any sense in cutting up a piece of material then sewing it back together again." I seem to recall that it was a very long day!

JESUS' EXAMPLE

We have a great example for using our time wisely. Jesus was a master at everything—time investment included. He had only three years for His ministry—talk about deadlines! He had goals that reached all the way to eternity. He balanced His days with fellowship with His friends, teaching, healing, praying, and fishing. He used "loose change" time for teaching. He certainly knew what His calling was; even as a 12-year-old He told His mother that He must be about His Father's business (Luke 2:49). Jesus even took time off. He spent much time in prayer, and often went alone to pray.

You don't have to be a supermom to have abundant life. Paul told the church at Colosse to "Let every detail in your lives—words, actions, whatever—be done in the name of the Master, Jesus, thanking God the Father every step of the way" (Colossians 3:17 *The Message*).

I love the story of the three men working on a project on the street corner. A fourth man approached them and asked the first, "What are you doing?"

"Laying bricks," came the reply.

"And what are you doing?" he asked the second man.

"Earning a living so I can feed my family."

"And you, what are you doing?" the third man was asked.

"Oh, sir, I'm building a cathedral to the glory of God."

Are you laying bricks, earning a living, or building a cathedral? The choice is yours.

CHAPTER ELEVEN

Supermoms

HAVE REMOTE CONTROLS

Have you ever watched a child (or an adult!) play with an electronic car that is operated by a remote control? The car turns corners, backs up, climbs over obstacles in the road, and changes direction, all at the command of the one holding the controls. Push a button, turn a knob—the car responds on cue.

A supermom sometimes finds herself wishing for remote-controlled children. The child's actions, words, and thoughts could be managed and corrected by a twist of a knob. No more embarrassing revelations in front of the teacher or company. You know, statements like, "Mama didn't really want company for supper, but Daddy had already invited you." No more temper tantrums in the grocery store; not even any more spilled milk in the restaurant. But how sad it would be if our children were little robots moving forward, to the side, over the obstacles in their path, all at our whim and command.

Of course, if we could have remote controls, wouldn't we enjoy some of the convenient features? You know, we could fast forward during the difficult stages. The teenager starts telling you how dumb you are, and how much you're damaging her reputation by making her stay home when "everyone else" is going to the party. Can't you just imagine pushing the fast forward button and watching casually as she finishes her tirade?

The reverse button would be nice, too. When we've blown it with our kids, we could rewind and do the whole scene all over again. Instant replay would give everyone a second chance to do it again, not making the same mistakes. Of course, we would probably make an entirely different set of mistakes, so we would need to keep rewinding until we finally got it right. Might wear out the rewind button before the warranty ran out on the remote control.

What about the mute feature? Just imagine looking earnestly into the face of your child, knowing what they are going to say even before they say it, and not having to hear it at all! We might also press the mute button on the preschooler when he starts telling the neighbor about the argument that you and your husband had the night before.

The pause feature would also be handy. It would give us time to think of the right response, time to make a decision. It might even give us time to take a nap while the rest of the world rushed on for a while. When Perry was in the third grade he had a very constant friend, one of those friends you finally have to tell when it's time to go home. I didn't know this until recently, but Perry told me that sometimes he would tell his friend, "I need to make a plan." Then he would crawl under the blanket on his bed, rest a few minutes, then come back out ready to play again. That would be using the pause button.

And of course we would want to use the record button for those scrapbook moments that are gone too quickly. Those are the times when you find your husband and your two-year-old asleep together on the sofa with the Dr. Seuss book on the floor nearby. Those are the times when you catch the first grader patiently "teaching" her little brother to read. Those are the times we'd like to record just for the sake of reference, like when the pre-teen says of her older sister, "I'll *never* act that way, Mama. I promise." Or perhaps we would like to record some situations so we could have time to process what is happening, then return to complete the scene later.

I guess we begin wanting to control, or at least influence, our children's behavior right from the start. That's not altogether a bad thing; they need to know what is expected of them, and what the standards are. We want our toddlers to smile at the right people and say "thank you" when they are supposed to. How many times have you heard a parent say, "Come on, honey, sing the song for them that you sing at home"? Then an apologetic, "They'll never do what you want them to in public." (Of course we never said that, did we?)

When Bob, Barbara, and their two boys came to our home for dinner I planned to make spaghetti. Most children like spaghetti, right? No, Barbara told me, her boys wouldn't eat that. I would need to fix them macaroni and cheese. Because I was a young mother myself, and because I wanted to be sure everyone was happy (that supermom thing, you know) I cooked both the spaghetti I had planned and a big bowl of macaroni and cheese. You've already guessed what the visiting boys ate, I'm sure. They never touched the macaroni, but devoured the spaghetti.

The expectations grow as the children grow. Making good grades in school, choosing the right friends, coming home five minutes before curfew, wearing the clothes and hairstyles that are acceptable to us—all these behaviors are indicators of a child with a "good" mother, right? If we could somehow just control by remote our children's environment, we could surely determine or at least influence the outcome.

One way of trying to maintain control is by asking children to make promises that we want them to keep even though they have no ownership of them. "Promise me you'll never do that." "Promise me you'll go to college and become a doctor." If we try to persuade them to make promises that we want them to keep, we are in reality trying to use that remote control on them, a remote control powered by a battery named *guilt*.

MOTHER BEAR

We human mothers could learn a lesson from Mother Bear. She spends the first year training Junior in their cozy little bungalow at 82 Many Berries Avenue. Then, when she is confident her offspring is ready to make it on his own, they plan an outing into the forest for a picnic. Once they have spread their picnic lunch beneath a tall pine tree, she suggests a fun game: she sends Junior up the tree on a scavenger hunt. Now here comes the difference between bears and humans—well, one of them. While Junior is happily occupied in the treetop, Mother quietly walks away, never to return. Junior climbed up the tree as a dependent cub; he came down an adult having to face life on his own.

We humans are much more sophisticated. Let's see, how would we approach this situation? Even if we sent our "cubs" up the tree, we would first give a list of instructions about how to climb, what to do while in the tree, and how to get back down. We would check on the progress of our children while they were in the tree, and we would be standing at the bottom, extending our hands to help them come back down safely to the ground. After practicing this routine a few times, we might eventually send the cub on a solo trip, but we would assure him that we would be back in the den if we were needed. We would be sure he had a cell phone so he could call us if he needed to, or more likely, if we wanted to check in on him. We want to be remote-control mothers, carefully monitoring and assisting in the developmental process.

Allowing our children to make mistakes is painful and unpleasant, but it is essential. We have a great example, you know. God allows His children to make mistakes. He began when He told Adam and Eve they had a choice. He stood by while they made a serious mistake in the Garden of Eden. Then He allowed them to experience the consequences of that mistake. A remote-control god would have pushed the lever or turned the knob just before Eve reached the tree, guiding her in a different direction than the one she was traveling. If God our Father, who is all-wise and all-loving, allows His children to make their own decisions and choose their own paths, I believe we should do the same, don't you?

I once read a mother's declaration that she had carefully tried to remove all the thorns from the roses so her daughter would not prick her finger. She carefully removed all the stones from the path so the daughter would not trip. Then she wrote, "But you still found thorns that caused you to bleed. You still found stones that caused you to stumble and fall." No matter how much we may want or try to make life "perfect" for our children, they must walk it by themselves.

My friend and his college son were working on the boy's car while he was home for the weekend. The boy insisted on doing things that seemed difficult or even ridiculous to the father. Finally, in exasperation, Dad said, "Son, *why* do you have to learn everything the hard way?"

"Dad, I want to learn them *my* way," he replied. Ouch!

BE IN CONTROL

But *some* control is necessary, of course. I recall a pastor telling about a home he was visiting where the little boy, an absolute terror, was obviously the one in control. My friend said he wanted to tell the mother, "If you'll give me five minutes with him, I'll give you back three!"

As parents it is our responsibility to discipline our children. Without that training, we have failed them and we will reap what we sow. "A refusal to correct is a refusal to love; love your children by disciplining them" (Proverbs 13:24 *The Message*). Child-rearing theories change almost as quickly as fashions. From Dr. Spock to Dr. Dobson, to tough love, and everywhere in between—a parent can become confused if they depend on the latest selling books and all the advice of well-intentioned friends. But one fact is sure: the opportunity to rear a child is a great gift and a great responsibility, and we must be good stewards of that gift.

TRAIN UP A CHILD

I wonder how many parents have claimed the promise that if they "Train up a child in the way he should go, and when he is old he will not depart from it" (Proverbs 22:6 NKJV)? Often it works that way; sometimes it doesn't. *The Message* gives us another look at that verse: "Point your kids in the right direction—when they're old they won't be lost." Because we don't have those remote controls, our children are free to make their own choices. Sometimes rebellious teenagers become responsible adults; sometimes they don't. One mother said that her daughter was six years old going on 20. Another mother responded that her daughter was 25 going on 14. Parents of adult children who have problems usually ask themselves, "Where did I go wrong? Was I too strict? Was I strict enough? Did I pray enough for them? Should I have done something different?"

Those are hard questions, and ones that really cannot be answered. Sure, all parents could have done some things differently. Sure, we all made mistakes. But for the most part we were doing the best we could. We must build a foundation of faith for our children, "point them in the right direction," then prayerfully send them into the world. And we must learn to forgive ourselves, keep our focus on our own Father, and trust His direction.

Jesus told us what kind of house we should build for ourselves, as well as for our children. "These words I speak to you are not incidental additions to your life, homeowner improvements to your standard of living. They are foundational words, words to build a life on. If you work these words into your life, you are like a smart carpenter who built his house on solid rock. Rain poured down, the river flooded, a tornado hit—but nothing moved that house. It was fixed to the rock. But if you just use my words in Bible studies and don't work them into your life, you are like a stupid carpenter who built his house on the sandy beach. When a storm rolled in and the waves came up, it collapsed like a house of cards" (Matthew 7:24–27 *The Message*).

MOTHER, NOT SMOTHER

Eugene Peterson says of the Proverbs 31 woman that "She keeps an eye on everyone in her household, and keeps them all busy and productive" (Proverbs 31:27 *The Message*). Again, "She looks well to how things go in her household" (AMP). Children want and need guidance. When they are teenagers and even as adults, they may still need us to be available to give encouragement, assistance, counsel, and support. But there is a difference in letting go and trying to control. I've always said that I want to be a mother, not a smother.

Karen, a fourth-grade teacher, and I were talking about our children and our desires to be mothers and not smothers. She told me about Todd, one of her fourth-graders. His mother walks him to school every morning, holding his hand. She is waiting at the school in the afternoon to walk him back home. Todd's teacher tells me that he talks baby talk, and he has difficulty relating to other children in the class. He is overly sensitive and cries a lot. Karen said, "Todd's mom is definitely a smother."

We talked in Chapter Five about the importance of teaching our children how to make their own decisions. That process should begin when they are very small, while we do still have some control and ability to guide them. We should always remember that they are individuals, not puppets. Yet we must step in at times and insure that the right decisions are made.

When his parents went out of town, we kept five-year-old David for a few days. He wanted to do something (I don't remember now what it was) that I would not let him do. He looked at me as though he couldn't believe I had said no. "But I *want* to," he explained patiently to me. I quickly realized that at home he was probably the one holding the remote controls.

As our children grow away from us, there are constant stages of adjustments as we lessen our control and allow them to take the lead. When they start to school, we no longer know what they are doing every minute of the day. Then when they become teenagers, they go out with friends in the evening. More letting go. Once they leave home there is a mixture of sadness because they are gone, concern that they are now on their own, and a sense of relief that even if we want to hold the remote control, it's now out of our hands.

Cindy's daughter graduated from high school with honors. Kristi went to college, played basketball, then in the summer after her second year faced a crossroads in her life. Should she go to nursing school or continue at the college where she was? She came home for a while to think about her decision.

Cindy's intentions were good—she was going to let Kristi make her own decision. She listened, but tried not give advice or suggestions. After about a week she sensed a lot of tension between the two of them. Finally a small disagreement flared into a full-scale argument, and Kristi burst into tears.

"*What* is wrong?" Cindy demanded.

"You don't even care what I do," Kristi sobbed. "I've tried to talk to you, but you won't even tell me what you think." She didn't want a remote-control mother, but she did want to know that the interest was still there.

With younger children it's often hard to know when to leave them alone or when to step in. Obviously, a poorly made bed is preferable to one not made at all. But sometimes we do need to help just a bit. One of my friends says that she asks her children, "Would you mind if I check this before we quit?"

We had access to several apricot trees while we lived at Shiprock. Every three or four years we had a bumper crop, and I canned apricot nectar, apricot butter, and made apricot jerky. Nita, then three, loved to help squeeze the juice from the apricots, but just wasn't strong enough to get out more than half the juice.

I hated to make her think she wasn't doing the job well, but I knew I had to squeeze them more. I thanked her for what she had done and said, "Now it just needs a mama-touch." She was satisfied, and still today says that some things need the mama-touch.

THE POWER OF TRUST

Before we feel confident in turning loose the remote control there must be trust. Being trusted by another person is both an honor and a great responsibility. Just before my daddy died he gave me power of attorney; I could go to the bank, post office, motor vehicle division, or anywhere else and sign his name followed by my name, POA. Jesus did that for us! He said that "whatever you ask *in My name,* that I will do, that the Father may be glorified in the Son. If you ask anything in My name, I will do it" (John 14:13–14 NKJV).

Do you practice trusting your children? Molly told me that the reason she never got in trouble when she was a teenager was that she knew her folks trusted her, and she must not disappoint them. If they know you trust them, your children will either respect the trust, or they will know there are serious consequences if they break that trust.

I often told my children never to tell me a lie or give me reason not to trust them. Once that trust was broken, they would have to work twice as hard to prove to me that I could trust them again. They tested that warning more than once, and discovered that my warnings were not just a threat.

Now another question: can your children trust you? That foundation of trust begins when they are very young. "If you do that again, I'm going to spank you." "Now, I told you already, if you do that again, I'm going to spank you." "Okay, I'm only going to tell you one more time—if you do that again, I *am* going to spank you." Really?

Can they trust you with their confidences? Stories of hurts, disappointments, and joys that are meant only for your ears don't need to be told to the world. When our three were small they each had their own room. I remember several times when I would put one child in bed and be told some big, important secret. Then when I would go to the next room that child would ask, "What did he tell you?"

I would reply, "If I tell you what he said, how do you know that I won't tell your secrets to him?" Now that they are adults, I hope they still know that what they tell me in confidence won't be told to anyone else.

A subtle way of holding on to the remote control even after our children have left the nest is to compare them with others or to criticize them. Sandy confided that she dreaded going to see her mother over the holidays. Why? "They don't like the way I'm raising my kids." I learned that whenever they are together, her mother alternately tells her that she is too strict or too indulgent, too demanding or too lenient. Sandy shouldn't give them snacks between meals, yet they can have snacks when they ask grandmother. Because Mom can't put down the remote control, she is forfeiting some precious times with her daughter's family.

Supermom can hold onto the remote control if she wants, but I much prefer letting my bear cubs become individuals. I prefer "building a house" for them that they can live in for the rest of their lives. For one thing, now that they are adults, I don't have the time or energy to control their lives. I do well to manage my own. Even if I were to try controlling them with subtle implications, they would still do what they wanted, and they would only resent me for trying to tell them what to do.

Sure, they make mistakes. So did I. And I still do! They do some things that I wish they wouldn't do; they do some that I would certainly do differently. But what joy it is to watch them as adults and know that I'm not responsible for every action, decision and choice they make. There is freedom in realizing that I don't have to hold the remote control in my hands—I just have to love them, and know that they love me.

CHAPTER TWELVE

Supermoms

WIN OSCARS

Have you ever watched several movies with one of your favorite actresses and been surprised that she could play so many different roles so well? One time she will be the heroine and the next time the witch. She may be a queen and then a pioneer mother. With each role she seemingly takes on a totally different personality. And when it's time for the Academy Awards, she wins an Oscar for at least one of those roles!

Look through a wide-angle lens at all the roles you play. You are mother, wife, sister, daughter, daughter-in-law, sister-in-law, neighbor, friend, teacher, employer, employee—movie stars have nothing on you, but I doubt that you have ever even been nominated for an Oscar! Our proverbial friend Miriam had many of these same roles: she was mother, wife, business-woman, homemaker, consumer, neighbor. More than likely she was also a daughter and perhaps a sister, aunt, neighbor, and friend. Let's look at some of the relationships 21st century mothers have and see what suggestions Miriam might have for us.

The most frequently mentioned role of the Proverbs 31 woman was that of wife. Keep in mind that this poem was written at a time when women were basically looked at as a man's possession. Her identity was found in her relationship to her husband. Look at the characteristics of a good wife that are mentioned in this chapter:

- Her husband can trust her (verse 11).
- She always treats her husband generously and without spite (verse 12).
- Because of her worthiness, her husband is greatly respected (verse 23).
- She is deserving of the public praise given to her by her husband. (verses 28–29).

Prior to this, the writer of Proverbs had already made several other statements about the husband/wife relationship.

- "A helpful wife is a jewel for her husband, but a shameless wife will make his bones rot" (Proverbs 12:4 CEV).
- "A man's greatest treasure is his wife—she is a gift from the LORD" (Proverbs 18:22 CEV).
- "A nagging wife goes on and on like the drip, drip, drip of the rain" (Proverbs 19:13 CEV).
- "You may inherit all you own from your parents, but a sensible wife is a gift from the LORD" (Proverbs 19:14 CEV).
- "It's better to stay outside on the roof of your house than to live inside with a nagging wife" (Proverbs 21:9 CEV).

I am not sure that Dalton would altogether agree with this last statement. He spent some time on the roof of our house once. While I wasn't a nagging wife, I was definitely preoccupied. It was a windy, cold March Saturday in western New Mexico. We had already had several snowstorms, and another was predicted for that day. He had noticed on Friday that a shingle had blown loose, and he wanted to replace it before the storm hit.

At 9:00 that morning he put some coffee on, went to the garage to get his tools, and headed for the roof. He hadn't been gone five minutes when the storm hit with a vengeance. It was snowing so hard that I could hardly see the car parked in front of the house. Boy, it's a good thing he got that shingle fixed, I thought, assuming that by this time he was working in the garage again.

Meanwhile, I was contented in my own warm world. I was working on a writing project while listening to my stereo. I washed one load of clothes and put them in the dryer, then put in another load to wash. I even had a couple of cups of coffee. About 10:30 I heard a persistent knock-knocking. Was my load of clothes off balance? No, everything was fine there. I went back to my writing. Still the knocking continued; I discovered that it was coming from the downdraft swamp cooler in the living room. (If you're not from the southwest you may not know what a swamp cooler is. When your annual rainfall is 12 inches, you add all the moisture to the air that you can!)

By now the snow had stopped, and I assumed Dalton was working on the roof again. Curious what he was doing, I decided to go check. When I opened the back door the first thing I saw was...his ladder. The wind had blown it over with that first snow. He had been on the roof all that time, calling down pipes, knocking on walls, trying every way possible to get my attention. He couldn't jump off the roof; it was too tall and he would have broken a leg for sure. No one was out in that kind of weather, of course, so no neighbors knew to come to his rescue. I quickly set up the ladder, and without saying a word he climbed down, put the ladder in the garage, and came inside.

I was trying my best not to laugh, because he obviously saw not one ounce of humor in the situation. Still shivering, he fixed himself a cup of coffee, then said his first words. "From now on, when I'm out like that, you come check on me every 15 minutes." He drank almost half his coffee in silence then added, "Make that every 10 minutes." By mid-afternoon he could smile again, and the next day he finally laughed about it all. But I know he would think twice as to whether or not it would be better to live on the roof than with a nagging wife!

MANY ROLES FOR MOMS

Does this mean that a woman is required to be a wife in order to be a good mother? Certainly not. I know so many single moms who are doing an outstanding job of rearing their children. A schoolteacher told me recently that only four of the 21 children in her class live in a home with both their birth mother and father.

Even when both parents do live in the same home, the home life may be far from ideal. Some parents are physically and/or emotionally abusive. They may be demanding, selfish, controlling. If one is a Christ follower and one is not, this can cause a lot of tension. Alcohol, poor money management, differing values, conflicting goals in life—all these things and many more can contribute to a difficult or unbearable marriage. And all these circumstances make mothering all the more challenging.

I have a question—where was the daddy in Proverbs 31? He was probably at city hall, playing checkers or whatever men played back then. Or perhaps he was actually taking care of business. Whatever, he gave her the freedom to run the house as she wanted, to be a businesswoman, and to make decisions on her own. It would certainly seem as though Miriam was the central figure in her home. Apparently, gathering from his praise of her in verses 28–29, he was appreciative of all her qualities.

Not all women are so fortunate. Perhaps someone could write a 32nd chapter for the book of Proverbs—"A truly good [husband] is the most precious treasure a [woman] can find" (adapted from Proverbs 31:10 CEV). What would we call that, the Superman Chapter? But of course that wouldn't work, because we all know that there really is a Superman—he's the mild-mannered newspaper reporter, Clark Kent.

I remember a five-frame cartoon I once saw. In the first frame the boss is yelling at the man/husband; in the second the man is scolding his wife. The third frame shows the wife/mother lecturing the son, and frame four pictures the boy scolding the dog. In the final frame the dog is chasing the cat. Amusing, but oh so true. No matter what has happened to us in the working world, no matter whether the marriage is healthy or unhealthy, children still need stability and godly parenting.

We have other family relationships also—other roles we live—and they can become very complicated. Many women today find that they have become part of the Sandwich Generation, dividing their time and energies between aging parents and children, balancing their roles as daughter and mother. Blended families, boomerang children who come back home, sometimes bringing a child or spouse, moving aging parents into the home—sometimes the supermom thinks she must be perfect in all of these relationships. It can be hard to admit that we cannot be "all things to all people," but we must also remember our priorities so we can maintain stability.

We also know that Miriam had other relationships outside her home. It would appear as though she was a good supervisor (verse 15). Surely her relationship skills enhanced her business abilities (verses 16 and 24). Maintaining healthy relationships is ideal but certainly not always easy.

Have you ever heard the expression that "It's hard to soar with eagles when you live with turkeys?" Lucy in the *Peanuts* comic strip says that she loves mankind—it's people she can't stand. I relate, don't you? There are some people in life who are easy to love—*some* people. No matter what you do, you should have done it another way. No matter how hard you try to please them, you never quite succeed. Joyce Landorf wrote a book several years ago called *Irregular People*. These are the ones whom I call sandpaper people. Some of them we can leave at work or the store; others we have to deal with on a daily basis.

KIDS NOT YOUR OWN

What about the kids next door? Have you ever wanted to lock the door and scream "No more! Go home!"? Perry had two Saturday morning friends—Bradley and Charley. We would wake up most Saturdays to find them sitting on the front porch. They weren't bad boys—they just weren't *my* children. But they ate cereal with Perry, watched cartoons with him, helped him feed the horses, and eventually went back to their home. Now, in retrospect, I wonder why it bothered me to have the boys there. I don't know where either of them are now, but I pray that being a part of our family for those few hours may have made a difference in their lives.

You can be a mother to other kids besides your own. In fact, many women who have never physically given birth to a child are as much or more "mother" than many birth mothers. Aunts, neighbors, teachers, babysitters, friends—many have filled the mother role in a very special way. Mother is sometimes as much a matter of the heart as it is of the womb.

For years I gave piano lessons in my home. On several occasions young people came for their lessons and left 30 minutes later not knowing much more about the G minor scale than when they came. But they left feeling a lot better because they had talked to someone about a problem they were having at school or at home.

I remember the Chocolate Bon-Bon cake I baked, and the would-be boyfriend who came to see Nita. She wasn't home yet, so I offered Brent a piece of cake while he waited. He left soon after Nita got there, but came back later that day for more cake! While he was there, I was able to share with him the difference Christ could make in his life.

Mothers need friends, too. Not just let's-have-lunch-some-time friends, though those are nice to have around when we need or want them. We need the kind of friend who helps us have garage sales and who sits with us in a hospital room while we watch a loved one die. The kind of friend who doesn't ask "What can I do to help?' but instead starts washing the dishes.

I have had some wonderful friends. Have you? Aren't you thankful for them? Cherish those friends you can laugh with, can tell how much you are hurting and they will cry with you, can tell about your mistakes and they don't hate you. They know you're not perfect. You know they aren't perfect, either. But you still love one another.

The writer of Ecclesiastes had such a friend, I'm sure, because he wrote, "You are better off to have a friend than to be all alone, because then you will get more enjoyment out of what you earn. If you fall, your friend can help you up. But if you fall without having a friend nearby, you are really in trouble. If you sleep alone, you won't have anyone to keep you warm on a cold night. Someone might be able to beat up one of you, but not both of you. As the saying goes, 'A rope made from three strands of cord is hard to break'" (Ecclesiastes 4:9–12 CEV).

Supermoms are great neighbors, too. "She's quick to assist anyone in need, reaches out to help the poor" (Proverbs 31:20 *The Message*). Haven't you known some people who are second-mile helpers? They don't wait to be asked; they seem to have a sixth sense about what needs to be done. Some have the gift of hospitality, opening their homes to others. Some are generous with what they have almost to a fault.

The Amplified Bible says that "She opens her hand to the poor, yes, she reaches out her filled hands to the needy [whether in body, mind or spirit]." Sometimes what people need is not tangible, and those "needy people" are all around us. Perhaps what they really need is a listening ear, a smile, or a hug. Peter and John had no money when a crippled man asked them for a handout. Peter replied, "I don't have a nickel to my name, but what I do have, I give you: In the name of Jesus Christ of Nazareth, walk!" (Acts 3:6 *The Message*). We assume that a single mother needs money when what she may really need is someone to watch her children for an evening so she can go shopping or to a movie. The checker at Wal-Mart needs a kind word of encouragement. Charlotte gave her pastor and his wife a priceless gift—she stayed with their three children while they went on a mini-vacation. I remember Mama baking bread for a sick neighbor, or taking cookies to a new family in the community.

Peter had some good words to say about this. "Love each other as if your life depended on it. Love makes up for practically anything. Be quick to give a meal to the hungry, a bed to the homeless—cheerfully. Be generous with the different things God gave you, passing them around so all get in on it: if words, let it be God's words; if help, let it be God's hearty help. That way, God's bright presence will be evident in everything through Jesus, and he'll get all the credit as the One might in everything—encores to the end of time. Oh, yes!" (1 Peter 4:8–11 *The Message*).

Another way we can "reach out our filled hands" is to mentor another mother. While we were in seminary Lorraine was my substitute mother. We never agreed that we would have a formal mentoring relationship. She just took a young mother under her wing, went with us to the hospital when our first two children were born, and taught me how to be a mother and wife as I watched her live her life with Ben and her five children.

What kind of relationship do you suppose Miriam had with her children? We really do not have many clues to answer that question. Proverbs 31:28 says that her children praise her (CEV), rise up and call her blessed (NKJV), and respect her (*The Message*). My neighbor says that these praises surely came from adult children; they probably didn't feel that way when they were young!

When do we become the "bad guy," laying down and enforcing rules? Can we be friends with our children, or must we maintain an authoritative role instead? My own relationship with all three of my children alternated between laughing, scolding, playing, disciplining, enjoying, and cautioning. I seriously doubt that we are much different from other mothers and their children.

A pastor/friend of mine told me about a conversation he had with his adult daughter who was having some problems with her teenager. My friend told her, "You cannot be friends with your children; you must be the parent instead." I'm not altogether sure I agree with him. Isn't there a balance between being the teacher, trainer, supervisor, and friend?

Of course the way we handle our relationships with our children depends on circumstances at the time, on the child, and on the situation. Erma Bombeck wrote to her children that "I loved you enough to say no even when you hated me for it." Part of the joy of being a grandmother and of having adult children is that you can enjoy the friendship relationship.

PLAYING GAMES

While Supermom surely does well in all of the relationships mentioned above, the rest of us need some help at times. Just as cars need tune-ups, so do relationships. Sometimes we play difficult games with those we should love the most. Games like checkers—I'm just waiting till you make a wrong move so I can jump on you. Or Scrabble—I'll take your words and make them mean something other than what you intended. We also play guessing games: guess who I am; guess who I want to be; guess why I am mad; guess what I want you to do. We play hide and seek—I will hide my emotions, you must find them. Or the "find the hidden meaning" variation: I said one thing, but I expect you to figure out what I really mean. There's even the game of Simon Says—if you don't say what I want you to say, you're out of the game. Our children are great learners. If they see us playing these games, they quickly join in and play along.

Our relationship with Christ should be natural. I heard a conference leader say that some people (I put supermoms in this category) want others to believe that they are "speeach-aal" (or however you would say *special*!). In other words, their spirituality is more for show and pretense than for real. Is she too good to be true? Yes! Goodness is its own advertisement. If someone tells you how humble she is, she isn't. If she goes into great detail about all she experienced during her daily quiet time, it wasn't very quiet.

Jesus had some very pointed words to say to those who parade their goodness. "Be especially careful when you are trying to be good so that you don't make a performance out of it. It might be good theater, but the God who made you won't be applauding. When you do something for someone else, don't call attention to yourself. You've seen them in action, I'm sure—'playactors' I call them—treating prayer meeting and street corner alike as a stage, acting compassionate as long as someone is watching, playing to the crowds. They get applause, true, but that's all they get. When you help someone out, don't think about how it looks. Just do it—quietly and unobtrusively. That is the way your God, who conceived you in love, working behind the scenes, helps you out. And when you come before God, don't turn that into a theatrical production either. All these people making a regular show out of their prayers, hoping for stardom! Do you think God sits in a box seat? Here's what I want you to do: Find a quiet, secluded place so you won't be tempted to role-play before God. Just be there as simply and honestly as you can manage. The focus will shift from you to God, and you will begin to sense His grace" (Matthew 6:1–6 *The Message*).

When the people heard Peter and John preaching they were amazed, and they realized that the two had been with Jesus (Acts 4:13). That is when we really shine—when others can recognize without our ever saying a word that we too have been with Jesus.

NO COMPARISON

There is something else we need to remember: even though we have so many roles to fill, we must still be true to the woman God created us to be. We must not allow ourselves to compare our abilities, limitations, circumstances, personalities, appearance, or anything else with others. Think of some men in the Bible who did this, and the consequences. Cain compared himself to Abel; the end result was God's disapproval and then Abel's murder. Esau's comparison of himself to Jacob, and vice versa, cost the two men years of happiness. When Saul compared himself to David he became so jealous that it destroyed his mind and cost him his kingdom. We can and must, however, compare ourselves to Christ. We are to focus on and try to emulate His attitudes, His teachings, His servant lifestyle.

Some of these relationships we choose; others are given to us. Some we can cultivate or ignore; some we must live with whether we want to or not. What gifts do you bring to those relationships in your life? What do you have in your hands? You may not have silver and gold, but you have so much to share with those who need you. "What you are doing is much more than a service that supplies God's people with what they need. It is something that will make many others thank God. The way in which you have proved yourselves by this service will bring honor and praise to God. You believed the message about Christ, and you obeyed it by sharing generously with God's people and with everyone else" (2 Corinthians 9:12–13 CEV).

CHAPTER THIRTEEN

Supermoms

HAVE PERFECT CHILDREN

At least, to hear them tell the stories, they must have perfect children.

"My child would *never* behave that way." (Interpretation: You must be a terrible mother to have a child who would do that.)

"Your daughter is *pregnant*?" (Interpretation: That would never happen to my daughter.)

"My son and his wife are so happy; they just bought a new house, you know. A little large for them, but it's just what they wanted. He has such a good job, and is sure to be promoted to manager soon."

Every time I see Mary she tells me what a *good* mother her daughter is. She goes on and on about her daughter's cooking, housekeeping, and parenting skills. She is critical of other mothers her daughter's age. Yet those of us who know both mother and daughter know that many of the mother's arrogant stories are not at all the way things really are at home. Her anecdotes are more fairytales than they are news reports.

The truth is, no one has perfect children, because guess what? They didn't have perfect parents! And their children's children aren't going to be perfect, either. We work under the mistaken illusion that if we are "average" mothers our kids won't amount to anything. It's our fault if they make Cs, if they get speeding tickets, marry the wrong person, or get fired from their jobs.

Isn't it just the highlight of your Christmas season when you get all those three-page Christmas letters? You know, the ones that begin, "Our children are just doing great. Johnny is getting his degree from Tech next spring. Mary has two beautiful children who love spending time at grandmother's house. Makes me wonder why I didn't have my grandchildren first!"

Translation: Johnny is finally, after eight years, about to finished his degree. We had to take time out for those extracurricular courses, the ones with names like Experiment with Drugs 101, Change Your Major (he repeated that class five times), Drop Out Mid-Semester 203, and those weekend seminars Party, Party, and Party More.

I had not seen Phyllis for several years when we met at a conference. "How are your boys?" I asked.

"Do you want the public version or the real version?" she asked. "Tim is in college and Steve has a good job working for the city. And I have the prettiest granddaughter you've ever seen!" Then she gave me the translation—Tim dropped out of college after one semester. He was in drug rehab after being arrested for selling marijuana. Now he's on probation with the stipulation that he goes back to school. Steve was married, but his wife filed for divorce after six months, and of course she got custody of their little girl.

Clair has three sons. When they were growing up, the older two were the "good kids" but the third son was always, it seemed, in some kind of trouble. Now they are all adults. The oldest son is married to a woman who prefers that her in-laws visit only when invited, which is usually once or twice a year. Rather than cause problems at home, he goes along with his wife. The second son has disappointed his parents by being party to some dishonest business dealings. Clair told me recently that the third son, who is a successful, happily married schoolteacher, said, "Well, Mom, I'll bet you never figured I'd turn out to be the good kid, did you?"

Another interesting thing about a supermom's children—they are never at fault. The preschooler was just protecting his territory when he hit the other child on the head with the baseball bat. In school he made poor grades because he had a bad teacher. He got blamed for causing trouble when it was his friend's fault. Even when he was not the little angel everyone was supposed to think he was, it was just mischievousness. After all, "boys will be boys, you know." He married a woman who was never good enough for him, so of course the marriage problems that resulted in divorce were totally her fault. Unfair supervisors and ridiculous company policies caused the problems he's having with his job.

The only reference to Miriam's children is that "her children praise her" (Proverbs 31:30 CEV) and "respect and bless her" (*The Message*). Otherwise their behavior is never mentioned. You see, bottom line is that we are responsible for ourselves, our own attitudes and conduct, our own lives. We are not responsible for the choices made by our children as they become adults. One of the most difficult parts of parenting adult children is admitting that they are humans who make their own decisions and mistakes, and who fail miserably sometimes.

What about those times when it really is your child's fault? When your child is the one who was wrong? When your child caused the divorce or committed the crime? That is hard to accept, and we want to take the responsibility for their actions. If we truly were supermoms when they were growing up, surely our children would be perfect, right?

I had not seen Anna for several years. As the mother of six now-adult children, she had experienced a lot of highs and lows on the parenting scale. She asked about my children, who were in middle and high school at the time. I replied, "Well, I'm almost afraid to say it, but at the moment, everything is great."

"Oh, just enjoy it while you can!" was her advice.

When our preschoolers are naughty, we discipline them in hopes of training them the right way. When they are in school we discipline in a variety of ways, still trying to help them develop into productive adults. They become teenagers and we are sure all hope is gone and our efforts were in vain. Then hopefully they emerge on the other side as pretty good people. Sure, they have faults and sometimes they don't make the grade. They fall down, but usually they get back up. They hurt and we hurt, but we all keep on going.

But what about those children who don't get back up? Jo's daughter had a baby while she was still in high school. She dropped out of school, left the baby with Jo, and disappeared for five years. When she finally came home, she took her daughter to another state where she was living with a man who physically abused her.

Barbara's daughter left her husband and their two young sons to "live out her dream" in Hollywood. She ended up on the streets as a prostitute and died from a drug overdose.

Deb's son was a high school teacher with a young family of his own. Her heart broke when he was arrested and sent to prison for sexually molesting several high school students.

I can only imagine that every one of these mothers, like millions of others, asked themselves the same questions: What did I do wrong? Where did I fail? What could I have done differently? What changes should I have made? I wonder if things would have turned out differently if I had only....

In Bill Cosby's book *Fatherhood* one chapter is titled, "The First Parent Had Trouble Too." "Whenever your kids are out of control, you can take comfort from the thought that even God's omnipotence did not extend to His kids." Then he tells in his own inimitable style the conversation between Adam, Eve, and the First Parent. He ends by saying, "There is reassurance in this story for those of you whose children are not doing well. If you have lovingly and persistently tried to give them wisdom and they haven't taken it, don't be hard on yourself. If *God* had trouble handling children, what makes you think it would be a piece of cake for you?"

ANDREW, THE PRODIGAL

In Luke 15:11–32 Jesus told a story about a man who was parenting a prodigal. We can learn so many helpful parenting lessons from the wise father in this parable. Since we've exposed the myth that our children are going to be perfect, let's see what help we can find in these verses.

The scene began when Andrew asked that he be given his portion of the inheritance. (You met Andy the prodigal son in chapter two.) Most 21st century children don't worry about their inheritance; their concerns are far less tangible. So when do we say firmly, "You're not old enough to have your inheritance"? How does the parent know when to hold on and when to let go? When do we tell our child, "This is your decision"? When do we offer our help? Someone has made the statement that there is no carpool to adulthood. That is one trip the child must make alone. We can only take her so far.

I wonder what happened in Andrew's home when he announced that he was claiming his inheritance. Did the father argue with his son, trying to convince him that this was not the thing for him to do? Did he suggest an alternative plan? Did he take Andy to a priest, or scribe, or friend for counsel? Did he try to persuade the boy with statements such as, "Why are you doing this to us? If you leave, it will break your mother's heart, you know." Whatever happened, we know that there surely was a great deal of tension in that home for a while.

Where did Andy go? Luke says that he went to a far-off land. I wonder where our children's far-off lands are. Sometimes they are what we consider pigpens but to them they are mud mansions or temporary stopping-off places. To the Jew the worst place to be was in a pigpen; to the Gentile the pig farm was just another place to make a living. Not the best job in the city, true; but not nearly as bad as it was to the Jewish family.

When Jackie dropped out of college to take a job at the local newspaper her parents were devastated. They knew their dreams for her future were hopeless. Ten years later when she was a well-paid, highly respected reporter for a large paper, their attitude had changed considerably. Kristi married her high school sweetheart during the Christmas break of their senior year; Jamie was born in June. Our children may not be who or what we want them to be, or dreamed that they might become. They make choices that determine their courses for the rest of their lives. So did we. Hopefully you have given them a foundation on which they can still build a future for themselves.

Remember that usually they haven't joined the pig-farmers union; this is probably just a temporary job. I'm sure that Andrew never forgot his pigpen days or, hopefully, the lessons he learned while he was there.

What do we do while we wait for them to come to their senses, or at least to recognize that there is another way of life? We can always do what Andrew's father did. He waited at home. He didn't saddle his donkey and set out to find the young man with plans of bringing him home. Instead, he sat on the rooftop, looking down the road, hoping and praying to see that familiar walk as his son came up the road.

Kenny Rogers' song "The Gambler" says, "You've got to know when to hold 'em, know when to fold 'em; know when to walk away, know when to run." How do we know when to wait for the prodigal to come home and when to go looking for him? There is no easy answer. Circumstances and personalities definitely affect our decisions. But we must remember that as children grow into adulthood they become responsible for their actions, and it is important that they realize that. If Andrew's father had found him there in the pigpen, he probably would have taken him to a motel where he could get a good bath, then taken him to the closest cafeteria for a good meal. But I daresay that in a day or two Andrew would have been right back living with those pigs again. He had to be the one to make the decision to leave.

Waiting is a terribly hard thing to do. Sitting in the living room at 4:00 A.M. listening for the crunch of tires on the gravel in the driveway; hoping every time the phone rings that it will be the call you've been waiting for, yet fearing that it might be the one you've dreaded; talking to your child but knowing that you're using entirely different dictionaries—there is no joy in any of these experiences.

Andrew did decide to do the right thing. He got so hungry that he was ready to pull corncobs from the pig slop and eat them. "That brought him to his senses," we are told, and he decided, "I'm going back to my father" (Luke 15:17–18 *The Message*). Good for Andrew. There is another possible scenario in this drama. Sometimes the prodigals get stuck in the mud at the pig farm and don't know when or even how to leave. What are we to do then? What if they don't ever leave that pigpen or if, by the time they want to leave, they are already so far into that lifestyle that there seems to be no way out? What if the scars are so deep or the consequences so permanent that they can't simply be left behind? That's when our hearts hurt, and we do all we can to help them. But we also must realize that we have to go on with our own lives and not move into the pigpen with them.

The first AIDS victim I personally knew was Shirley's son. He had been living in Europe for several years when he called home to tell his folks he was gay and that he was dying. I shall never forget the day Shirley told me this news. Her world crumbled around her. What to do? No, he didn't want to come "home." He wanted to stay in Europe and die there. Shirley flew to see him, spent a few weeks by his side, then came back home, leaving him to die in the home of his lover. Shirley's heart was broken, of course, but after grieving she moved on, determined to live the rest of her life to the fullest and not let her son's mistakes destroy her life, too.

But Andrew came home! We've heard the story so many times that most of us have created this beautiful image in our minds. Dad sees Andy coming up the road, calls out to everyone in the house, "He's coming!" then runs out and gives the wanderer a big bear hug. He doesn't listen to Andy's explanations or apologies; he even tolerates the pigpen aroma emitting from Andy's soiled clothes. He goes into action planning a huge homecoming celebration.

Guess what? Not all homecomings are quite so glorious. She may come home with a child or a drug addiction. He may come home because the car wreck left him permanently in a wheelchair. Just because they're home doesn't mean the drama has ended. There may be some deep emotional scars that will take time to heal, if they ever do. Angry words may have created deep chasms that need to be bridged.

The fatted calf still needs to be barbequed, even if it is not served all at the same time. Celebrations may not come spontaneously; they may come after tiny little victories. Just let the child know you love him; tell him you're cheering him on. Affirm successes and don't dwell on defeats. Remember, fatted calves are really just symbols of forgiveness. When God says, "I forgive you," He does it completely.

Don't demand of yourself that you be a supermom in these situations, either. You also have some hurts that need healing. You have some wounds that need to be cleaned out before they get infected. You had to adjust to a situation that you never signed up for. You had to live through some nightmares when you wanted to wake up, then realized you were awake. It's okay to admit that you need help, whether it is from a counselor or a good friend with soft shoulder pads and a box of tissues.

And they all lived happily ever after, right? Not! Just when Daddy thought things were going to be okay, here comes big brother Ben. Haven't we all been there? Just before one crisis is past another one pops up. Ben stuck out his bottom lip and whimpered, "Look how many years I've stayed here serving you, never giving you one moment of grief, but have you ever thrown a party for me and my friends? Then this son of yours who has thrown away your money on whores shows up and you go all out with a feast!" (Luke 15:29–30 *The Message*).

Don't you just love it? No matter how hard you try—how many times you think you've explained it—they still don't get it! Again we have a wise father's example we can follow. He didn't treat both sons the same way. He might have said, "Okay, son, just to reward your faithfulness I'm going to give you a party next Saturday night." Or he might have told Ben how wrong he was to feel slighted—might have told him, "You can't feel that way." Instead Father affirmed the older son for his faithfulness and openly, honestly confronted the issue at hand.

I heard about a grandmother who brought water pistols when she went to visit her daughter and grandsons. The daughter said, "Mom! I can't believe you did that. Don't you remember how much grief we gave you with our water pistols?"

Grandmother smiled sweetly. "Yes, dear, I do!"

So, do supermoms have perfect children? Probably so, if you listen to their accounts. Meanwhile, the rest of us can celebrate the victories, pray through the rough times, and be thankful for those imperfect, wonderful children God entrusted to our care. And when they are grown and have imperfect children of their own, we can smile sweetly and say, "Yes, dear, I understand!"

CHAPTER FOURTEEN

Supermoms

DON'T GROW OLD

Supermoms not only don't die; they don't even grow old. Now if that doesn't completely destroy any illusions you may have had that you are a supermom, just look in the mirror! The really disturbing thing you discover when you go to high school reunions is how old all your friends have become. Botox, Oil of Olay, liposuction, hair color, and facelifts—they still can't change the inevitable fact that we all grow old. And as my friend Dean says, "Growing old is better than Plan B!" Ultimately we all grow old if we live long enough. I heard someone say recently that life is like a roll of toilet paper—the closer you get to the end, the faster it goes.

My pastor told about a woman who lived to be 100. (You've heard of her before, haven't you?) A reporter asked what factors had attributed to her long life. "I went to bed early, got up early, didn't drink or smoke, and exercised every day."

The reporter responded, "My uncle did the same thing, but he died when he was 54. What do you say about that?"

"He just didn't do it long enough," she replied.

Marie, age 84, saw a friend she had gone to high school with, but had not seen since graduation. "You look just like you did back then," the friend said. Marie thought, *Oh, dear, have I always looked this old?*

SHE REJOICES OVER THE FUTURE

Proverbs 31:25 tells us that "She rejoices over the future [the latter day or time to come, knowing that she and her family are in readiness for it]" (AMP). Fear of or worry about the unknown is one of the most non-productive uses of our energies. Jesus asked His followers, "Has anyone by fussing in front of the mirror ever gotten taller by so much as an inch? All this time and money wasted on fashion—do you think it makes that much difference? Instead of looking at the fashions, walk out into the fields and look at the wildflowers. They never primp or shop, but have you ever seen color and design quite like it? The ten best-dressed men and women in the country look shabby alongside them....Give your entire attention to what God is doing right now, and don't get worked up about what may or may not happen tomorrow. God will help you deal with whatever hard things come up when the time comes" (Matthew 6:27–29, 34 *The Message*).

While supermoms aren't afraid of the future, we reality moms do have our fears. It may be growing old, or sickness, or financial insecurity, or being left in an empty nest after our children leave, or retirement, or simply fear of the unknown. What unknowns in the future are you afraid of? What can we do about those fears that keep us from enjoying the "abundant lives" that we are supposed to live?

Worrying about growing old is really pointless, you know. If we have a fear of growing old, perhaps we need to ask ourselves why we are afraid. Is it in reality a fear of sickness, or dependence, or loss of abilities we now enjoy? I watched my mother die from breast cancer. I hope I don't have cancer, of course, but I don't fear cancer like I do some other things that might be in my future. One of my friends says that 95% of what we worry about never happens, so he's decided it's a good idea to worry!

Shea's grandmother was one of those I'll-never-grow-old women. At 78 she weighed 125 pounds and was still active and attractive. When she came for a visit, Shea made a German chocolate cake, her favorite. Grandmother only ate one piece; she had to watch her weight, you know. Soon after Grandmother went back home she discovered that she had terminal cancer; five weeks later she was dead. Shea never saw her again. "Why didn't she go ahead and enjoy the cake?" Shea wondered.

I can't keep myself from growing old, but I can keep myself from growing bitter. I can do the best I can to take care of my body and my mind. I can prepare for the future. And I can keep an attitude of gratitude for today, remembering that every day is a gift from God. I can determine that each day I will become more like the Master.

Paul gave some wonderful advice to the church at Philippi. "Don't fret or worry. Instead of worrying, pray. Let petitions and praises shape your worries into prayers, letting God know your concerns. Before you know it, a sense of God's wholeness, everything coming together for good, will come and settle you down. It's wonderful what happens when Christ displaces worry at the center of your life" (Philippians 4:6–7 *The Message*).

Though my paternal grandmother, we called her "Mom," was 98 when she died, I don't think she ever knew that she was old. When she was 88 she showed me a pattern for a beautiful velvet quilt. "I think I'll make one of those when I am old," she told me.

On her 95th birthday several of her family gathered for a birthday party. After it was over she gave me a beautiful, intricate 2' by 2' sample quilt square she had recently made. I was amazed at the detail and precision; it was truly a work of art. Many hours of labor had gone into just this one block. "You might as well have this," she said. "I don't think I'll ever get a quilt like this made."

At 96 her doctor suggested that she might want to use a walking cane as she worked in the small yard in front of her retirement apartment. "I don't want to use this thing. People will think I'm old," she complained.

On a flight one time I sat beside a woman who had just celebrated her 70th birthday. She said, "I don't mind being 70. But I just don't know how I got there so fast."

I called my Aunt Corrine on her 80th birthday. "Eighty used to sound old, but it doesn't really sound that old any more," I said, trying to be encouraging.

"Oh, honey, it sounds old to me!" she exclaimed.

My friend Selma has cerebral palsy. Though her physical body is terribly limited, her mind is sharp. In fact, she has a college education and has taught school. For years she arrived at church an hour early so she could go into a small room to pray. Now, as her tiny, tired body is wearing out, she spends all her days in a wheelchair, at the mercy of others to help her. The last time I saw her she told me in her halting way, "I don't know why God lets me keep on living."

I hugged her and said, "Because we need you to pray for us." I don't know if that answer made any difference to her or not, but I needed her to know that she still was important to us.

I've always been amazed at how God prepares us just in time for what is ahead. When our children are toddlers completely dependent on us, we can't imagine life without them in our homes. Our family enjoyed some special summer vacations.

I can remember thinking, "How can I enjoy a vacation without my children? Will it even be fun?" I've discovered that it's quite fun! Someone has said that God gives us teenagers to prepare us for the empty nest!

HOW DO YOU SEE YOURSELF?

It is interesting to note that this verse comes toward the end of this 31st chapter. When we are young, active, and very much alive, old age is far away. It's not reality. We are invincible! Surely we will never need a walking cane, nor have spider veins on our legs. Oh sure, our heads tell us that old age is out there somewhere, waiting for us. But it is such a long way away that we don't have to be too concerned.

Then one day we look in the mirror and find our mother looking back at us. We see wrinkles around our eyes and gray hair framing our face. Our parents and their siblings die, and we realize that we are the last generation. We realize that the middle-aged woman who lived across the street when we bought our house is now an old woman. If that could happen to her, could it happen to us?

A man told his friend, "Your wife is as beautiful as ever."

"Yes," the husband replied, "but it takes her a lot longer to get that way."

Our self-perception is such an interesting illusion. One month before his 80th birthday my daddy announced that he was getting married again to a 76-year-old woman. His sisters listed all the reasons he shouldn't marry at his age. He listened patiently to them, then said thoughtfully, "Well, there's one thing about it. If it doesn't work out, it *can't* last too long!"

A friend of my about-to-be step mom kept looking at me during the wedding. During the reception she said, "I am sure I know you."

"Well, I grew up here," I replied. "We've probably met somewhere."

A little later she pursued the thought. "I just know that I know you. Maybe we went to school together." Now you understand, this woman was my stepmother's age; either she or I were way off base in the way we thought we looked. After the third attempt I excused myself and went to the bathroom to check my makeup. Maybe I had forgotten to put on any? No, all was normal.

I went back to the reception, hoping that was the end of the story. Oh, no, here she came again. "I just *know* we had to have gone to school together."

"What year did you graduate?" I finally got up enough courage to ask. Twenty-four years before I did! *Twenty-four years!* Her son and I graduated together! It may have made her feel better to think she looked 24 years younger than she was, but it sure didn't do anything for my psyche to think I might look 24 years older!

Before Oneta had cataract surgery she didn't realize how gradually her eyesight had been regressing. After she had the surgery she was looking down at her hands when the doctor removed the bandages from her eyes. She told me that she actually jumped and pulled her hands back when she saw them. The last time she saw her hands, they were young and firm; now they were the hands of an old woman.

Have you ever noticed how much our mailboxes are indicators of the calendars of our lives? When we are first married we receive wedding announcements from our friends, then come Christmas cards telling about their new homes and new jobs. Next we receive birth announcements, followed by cards telling about the children's accomplishments, graduations, marriages, and children. Suddenly we are receiving invitations to 50th wedding anniversaries and retirement celebrations.

Then the Christmas card tells of the death of a spouse or the battle with a disease.

Growing old is just one of the things we can worry about. Haven't you known people who worry for no reason? Remember Richard Carlson's book, *Don't Sweat the Small Stuff...and It's All Small Stuff*? Pretty good advice!

Paul had some good advice, too: "Don't fret or worry. Instead of worrying, pray. Let petitions and praises shape your worries into prayers, letting God know your concerns. Before you know it, a sense of God's wholeness, everything coming together for good, will come and settle you down. It's wonderful what happens when Christ displaces worry at the center of your life" (Philippians 4:6 *The Message*).

Worry is one of the most non-productive ways we can invest our energies. We don't have to be supermoms to remember that "greater is He that is in me than he that is in the world." A friend of mine ends all her emails with this quote: "Don't tell God how big your mountains are. Tell your mountains how big God is."

WHERE DO YOU LIVE?

Again I remember the Scripture about a "tree planted by the rivers of water" (Psalm 1:3 NKJV). The plains and farmlands of eastern New Mexico do have trees; we just don't have an over-abundance of them. When you drive 30 or 40 miles and never see a tree, you don't complain, you just enjoy a tree when you do see one. Some trees have grown for decades, and are still standing strong. You can tell which way the prevailing winds blow by the way the tree leans. Many kinds of trees bend and wave with the wind, but some others, like pine and poplar trees, are rigid. They snap and break when strong winds push against them.

Women who make God the focal point in their lives are like those trees that bend and sway when the winds blow. The winds may shape their lives to an extent, and you may even be able to trace the lines of the storms on their faces. But they have allowed the Heavenly Father to prune and shape them into beautiful, fruit-bearing trees. They won't break when the winds are strong; they stand tall knowing God is in control.

I received a letter from my friend Margie awhile after she had been diagnosed as having Alzheimer's disease. One sentence in the letter changed my life. She wrote, "It's a good day when I wake up and know who I am and where I live."

I thought, *Every day we should remember who we are and where we live.* Who am I? I am a woman created in the image of God. I have been given the beautiful gift of life. There are many things I can't do; there are many things I can do. There are some things I can change about myself; there are some things about me that the world and I just have to deal with. I have the opportunity to touch those around me and hopefully to leave footprints and fingerprints that will make a difference.

Where do I live? I live in a world that has been shaped in part by circumstance, in part by others in my life, and in part by me. I've made mistakes, and will make more, but I've tried to do the best I could. I live with the consequences of some mistakes, but I've tried to learn lessons from them and move on. My sins have been covered, washed away by the blood of the Lamb. Where do I live? I live in my Father's love!

Yes, Margie, it's a good day when we remember who we are and where we live. So you're worried about growing old? Get over it! Capture the wonder and mystique of today. And remember, when our focus is on our Father, truly the best is yet to come.

CHAPTER FIFTEEN

Supermom

HAS LEFT THE
BUILDING

And in her place is a real, live Proverbs 31 mother living in a
21st century world—a woman who is "worth far more than
diamonds" (Proverbs 31:10 *The Message*), than "precious
gems" (TLB), and "the most precious treasure a man can find"
(CEV). I like being compared to a precious gem, don't you?

Think about the value of gems when this poem was orig-
inally written. Records show that silver was used as a medium
of exchange even in the time of Abraham. As humans devel-
oped a more cultured society, certain gems gained recognition
as having more worth than others. Scarcity and hardness of
the stone primarily determined its value. Next to be considered
were more subjective qualities: intensity and shade of color,
shape, general beauty. By the time of the writing of Proverbs,
the values of certain gems were definitely established, and
the possession of a priceless gem was counted to be not only
financially beneficial, but a mark of social distinction as well.

So what makes a gem "beautiful"? Many qualifications
are considered when appraising the value of a gem. The most

valuable diamond may be lovely to look at, but probably not as lovely in the eyes of a young woman as a simple pearl set in gold and given to her by her sweetheart. Fashion likewise dictates qualifications of beauty. A diamond has classic beauty, but its settings will vary from elaborate gold trim to a simple silver band, dependent on the fashion mood of the day. At one time turquoise was considered to be of relatively insignificant value. Then jewelry made by the American Indians began to find a worldwide market, and almost overnight turquoise became one of the most demanded stones on the American scene. A jeweler tells me that we might consider all gems as precious if they are desirable and in demand.

Each gem has its own characteristics. The mineral content, number of impurities, and degree of hardness vary from stone to stone. The impurities in a ruby are what give the stone its brilliant color. The opal is of such soft texture that only its superior fire and astonishing play of color qualify it to be classed as a gem. Special care must be taken to prevent abrasion or fracture of this stone.

I have read that more than 80 percent of the world's diamonds are not ornamental—they are industrial. Diamonds are one of the hardest materials. They are used to cut materials that other abrasives cannot cut. Think of the women you have known. Haven't more of them been industrial diamonds than ornamental ones? When I think of industrial diamonds I think of women like Sally. For more than 20 years she and her husband managed a camp in New Mexico's Sacramento Mountains. There is no way to count the number of mornings she crawled out of her warm bed to prepare dozens and dozens of cinnamon rolls for hungry campers. She made quilts for the beds in the motel, was active in her church, and had time to rear her five children. One child is now in medical school, one has almost completed her Ph.D. in church history, one is a pastor, one a missionary, and one co-directs the camp with her parents.

I think of women who have gone before us, women like my mother-in-law. She, her husband, and their two young sons moved to New Mexico in a covered wagon. She gave birth to seven more children; one daughter died when she was just a few days old. Hammah didn't finish high school; she never traveled far from home. Her small adobe house with potted geraniums sitting in the windowsills would never have been featured in *Better Homes and Gardens*. Yet this industrial diamond left a legacy of resilience, strength, and determination for the generations that followed her.

It's not important that every woman be a diamond of distinction; it is rather that she be beautiful in her environment. Whatever your setting, whatever type gem you may think you are, be a precious gem for Him. The word *beauty* can have many interpretations. Peter's advice to women was, "Don't depend on things like fancy hairdos or gold jewelry or expensive clothes to make you look beautiful. Be beautiful in your heart by being gentle and quiet. This kind of beauty will last, and God considers it very special" (1 Peter 3:3–4 CEV).

One of the most amazing things about the humans God created is that every one of us is unique! Have you ever sat in an airport and watched all the shapes and sizes, faces and feet that pass you? Surely God must have had fun thinking of all the different personalities who would make up the world. Really the world would be a rather dull place to live if we were all alike. (Of course, there are some people we know on whose personalities we might like to make a few alterations—but that's another book!)

The beauty of God's plan is that we do not have to fit into a certain mold to be "right." He intended us to be the very best of just what He created us to be. When Paul wrote to the church at

Ephesus, he reminded them that it is God Himself who made us what we are and gave us new lives from Christ Jesus (Ephesians 2:10). If you work, do your very best. If you sing, make beautiful music. If you are an artist, paint beautiful pictures.

You don't have to be just like anyone else; just be the best woman you can be.

The children of the Proverbs 31 mother "respect and bless her" (verse 28 *The Message*). Have you blessed your mother lately? Have you thanked her for all that she did for you? I was just a young mother when Mama died, so I really didn't know her after I was an adult. But her influence in my life is indelible. I still have her Bible and often, when I need to be reminded of one of God's promises, I look at those worn pages and find some that she highlighted. When I look in my guest room I see her treadle sewing machine and remember how patiently she taught me many of the lessons of life that still guide me today. When I play the piano I'm thankful that she taught me how to play, and when I sing familiar hymns I'm thankful that she sang them to me when I was a child, and that she gave me a firm foundation of faith.

Mama had planned her funeral several weeks prior to her death. As Betsy's voice rang out clearly it was as though Mama herself was singing her final testimony for those of us left behind.

All the way my Savior leads me;
  oh, the fullness of His love!
Perfect rest to me is promised in my Father's house above:
When my spirit, clothed immortal,
  wings its flight to realms of day,
this my song thro' endless ages: Jesus led me all the way;
this my song thro' endless ages: Jesus led me all the way.

We read about some special mothers in the Bible. I can only imagine how hard it was for Moses' mother to place him in that basket and set it afloat on the river. What about Hannah, leaving Samuel, the son she had longed for, at the temple with Eli the priest? What love must have gone into the new clothes she made each year to take to this special child (1 Samuel 2:19). Think about the faith passed down from Mother Eunice and Grandmother Lois to Timothy (2 Timothy 1:5).

Even though we idealize and romanticize Mary, the mother of Jesus, she was just a woman. That is part of the beauty of the humanity of Christ. I wouldn't be surprised if she didn't get impatient with her children just as we do. Do you remember the time her twelve-year-old Son stayed behind in Jerusalem, visiting with the teachers and asking them questions? We can surely identify with her when, after searching for Him for three days, she asked, "Young man, why have you done this to us? Your father and I have been half out of our minds looking for you" (Luke 2:48 *The Message*). Then I love the statement in verse 51. "His mother kept all these things in her heart" (NKJV). A mother's heart is such a treasure trove of memories and dreams, secrets and surprises.

Were all these ladies supermoms or just plain women doing the best they could—faithfully doing what they knew God asked of them? I believe they were ordinary women that God used in extraordinary ways. There have been millions of other ordinary mothers through the ages who have touched the world around them in gentle ways as they faithfully walked through each ordinary day, obediently following God. Without each mother training, teaching, praying, encouraging, washing, cooking, praying, cleaning, crying, laughing, and praying some more, the world would not be a very good place to live.

Biological mothers are not the only ones who have "mothered" the next generation. Let's not forget all those aunts, grandmothers, friends, sisters, teachers, and babysitters who have guided a child's life. Mothering is more than a biological process; it is also a matter of the heart. Not too long ago we heard the reminder that it takes a community to rear a child. Many women who never actually gave birth have nonetheless been nurturers to others' children. Thank you to all those women who take the time to invest themselves in the life of a child.

EACH DAY IS A GIFT

Twenty-first century mothers, celebrate the days, the hours, the moments that God has given to you as a gift. Be yourself, and live like the child of the King that you are. Live each day with anticipation and joy. We make plans for life's big mile markers—weddings, births, career changes. Yet we come upon many great events purely by accident. We chance to meet a person and our lives are changed forever. We choose to walk on a side trail and our lives are never again the same. We are in an accident and receive a wound that takes a lifetime to heal. We say "yes" to a new challenge and a world of opportunities becomes ours. We see a flower, stop to smell it, and discover it is one of the rarest flowers in the world. We say "I'll see you tomorrow" and never see that friend again. People went to a ball game in San Francisco and sat through an earthquake. Hundreds were watching a parade when a shot rang out, and the President was dead. A small band of shepherds were watching their sheep one night, and they heard the angels sing the first Christmas cantata.

I pray that my eyes will stay open so I will recognize these moments when they come—that each day I will feel excitement and anticipation, for every moment, every day may be one of the best, the grandest that I have yet lived.

"Life is like a piano. What you get out of it depends on how you play it." When I saw this framed inscription in our minister of music's office I immediately thought of the implications the idea has for women as we live in the 21st century. Then I wrote this in my journal:

Life, like the piano, must be played with expression to be effective. Play allegro sections quickly, with joy and enthusiasm, yet smoothly. When playing rubato, change the rhythm to express yourself. Know when to crescendo and decrescendo. Move lightly over staccato notes; linger and savor the largo movements. Don't be afraid to play forte. Or even fortissimo. But know when to change from forte to piano. Or pianissimo.

No matter how many hours are spent in practice, no one ever reaches perfection. Even those who have natural ability must practice in order to do their best. Some practice is fun; much practice is tedious and repetitious and difficult—working to correct mistakes, to conquer difficult passages.

Learn the terms, the direction, so you will be able to play the piece as the Composer intended. Don't be afraid to try new pieces, new challenges. It may not be your style, but don't rule it out, don't put away the book, till you try. Enjoy old pieces. Play your favorite songs again. And again. And again. Improve on them. Memorize them. Feel satisfaction with your accomplishments. Play a variety of songs—classical, religious, ragtime, popular. Learn to appreciate diversity.

There is a big difference between practice and performance. When practicing, you establish good patterns so that you don't even think about them when performing. You repeat difficult passages over and over until you can play them correctly when performing. You play them slowly at first, then gradually faster and more smoothly until they become your friend. By accepting the disciplines of practice, the musician becomes ready for the performance. Good habits pay off. Fingering, hand position, body posture, pedal control—all combine to make the performance so much better. When you play a wrong note while practicing, stop. Find out what is wrong. Correct it. When performing, go on. Don't stop.

Make the most of every song, every movement, every note. There will be some passages you don't really like. Play them as if they were your favorite. Even minor keys—especially minor keys—can be the most beautiful of all. Even if the song you are playing may never be heard by anyone else, play it as though you were performing for the King. Whenever you can, share your song with someone else. For playing the piano and living life—both are meant to be shared.

Long ago I gave up my ambitions of becoming the World's Greatest Supermom. My socks don't always rhyme. I have spots on my drinking glasses and rings around my collars. I yell when I should be quiet; I pout when I should confront. I lock my keys in the car, make lumpy gravy, and burn the toast. I have spider webs on my ceiling and dust on my baseboards. My hair turned gray, my face got wrinkled, my mental memory chip needs to be rebooted frequently.

I've discovered that some days I just don't feel very super, and that I am *not* super more times than I *am* super. And when I do come close to being super, God gets the credit. But when I told Rhonda that I was writing a book about supermoms, she hugged me and said, "That's good, Mom, because you are one.

But you are also real." I think I'll choose real over super any day, won't you?

You can go ahead and claim to be a supermom. You'll have no friends, you realize. Even if some think you are "super," they will probably avoid you because you remind them they are not perfect. Some will see right through you—they know the truth that there is no such thing as a perfect woman. And besides, no one will really care.

When supermom leaves the building, the washing machine will still eat one sock. You buy a coat for $75 one week, then find it on sale a week later for $25. You may still be no faster than a water pistol, no stronger than a model train. When you try to leap those tall buildings, you may hang your toe and fall flat on your face! But when you give up control of yourself and turn your life over completely to the leadership of God, you are the best kind of superwoman! "Charm can mislead and beauty soon fades. The woman to be admired and praised is the woman who lives in the Fear-of-God. Give her everything she deserves! Festoon her life with praises!" (Proverbs 31:30–31 *The Message*).

Do you know what's really wonderful? Even though our families, the world, and we ourselves try to put mothers into this impossible role, *God* does not require us to be supermoms! He understands when we fall down. He forgives us when we make mistakes. He loves us in spite of our faults. He wants us have an abundant life, and He is available to free us, to help us have that life. He was talking to mothers, too, when He said "I came so they can have real and eternal life, more and better life than they ever dreamed of" (John 10:10 *The Message*).

Paul wrote, "I've learned by now to be quite content whatever my circumstances. I'm just as happy with little as with much, with much as with little. I've found the recipe for being happy whether full or hungry, hands full or hands empty. Whatever I have, wherever I am, I can make it through anything in the One who makes me who I am" (Philippians 4:11–13 *The Message*).

Oh, we still make mistakes, do dumb things, say things we shouldn't. We don't become perfect, but we enjoy our privileges as daughters of the King. We are given the key to His storehouse. We become joint heirs with Jesus! We know He will hold our hand when we walk on the mountaintop and in the valley, down crowded streets and grocery store aisles, through cluttered bedrooms, in the office where we work, beside a hospital bed, down paths we've never walked before—and paths where we'd rather not walk.

Talk about super! How much more *super* can we be? With our faith placed wholly in Christ Jesus, we have access to life's richest treasures. The writer of Hebrews reminds us that "The fundamental fact of existence is that this trust in God, this faith, is the firm foundation under everything that makes life worth living. It's our handle on what we can't see" (Hebrews 11:1 *The Message*). What we need, according to God's best plan for our lives, is what He promises to give us. When we as mothers put Christ first in our lives, truly make Him Lord of all, that's when we come closest to being the best kind of supermom.